RESIST MUCH
OBEY LITTLE

RESIST MUCH
OBEY LITTLE

REMEMBERING ED ABBEY

Edited by James R. Hepworth

and Gregory McNamee

SIERRA CLUB BOOKS · SAN FRANCISCO

The Sierra Club, founded in 1892 by John Muir, has devoted itself to the study and protection of the earth's scenic and ecological resources—mountains, wetlands, woodlands, wild shores and rivers, deserts and plains. The publishing program of the Sierra Club offers books to the public as a nonprofit educational service in the hope that they may enlarge the public's understanding of the Club's basic concerns. The point of view expressed in each book, however, does not necessarily represent that of the Club. The Sierra Club has some sixty chapters coast to coast, in Canada, Hawaii, and Alaska. For information about how you may participate in its programs to preserve wilderness and the quality of life, please address inquiries to Sierra Club, 85 Second Street, San Francisco, CA 94105.

Copyright © 1996 by James R. Hepworth and Gregory McNamee.
Individual selections are copyrighted by their respective authors.

LIBRARY OF CONGRESS CATALOGING-IN-PUBLICATION DATA
Resist much, obey little : remembering Ed Abbey / edited by James R.
Hepworth and Gregory McNamee.
p.   cm.
Includes bibliographical references.
ISBN 0-87156-879-9 (pbk. : alk. paper)
1. Abbey, Edward, 1927–1989. 2. Abbey, Edward, 1927–1989—Interviews.
3. Authors, American—20th century—Interviews. 4. Western stories—
Authorship. 5. West (U.S.) in literature. I. Hepworth, James, 1948– .
II. McNamee, Gregory.
PS3551.B2Z85   1996
813'.54—dc20   96-17160

Production by Robin Rockey · Cover photograph by Jack Dykinga
Cover and book design by Amy Evans
Composition by Wilsted & Taylor

Printed in the United States of America on acid-free paper containing
a minimum of 50% recovered waste paper of which at least
10% of the fiber content is post-consumer waste.
10   9   8   7   6   5   4   3   2   1

Wilderness is not a luxury but a necessity of the human spirit, and as vital to our lives as water and good bread. A civilization which destroys what little remains of the wild, the spare, the original, is cutting itself off from its origins and betraying the principle of civilization itself.

EDWARD ABBEY, *Desert Solitaire*

Contents

Preface   *xi*

Wendell Berry
A Few Words in Favor of Edward Abbey   *1*

William Eastlake
A Note on Ed Abbey   *15*

Gregory McNamee
Scarlet "A" on a Field of Black   *18*

Jack Loeffler
Edward Abbey, Anarchism, and the Environment   *31*

Luis Alberto Urrea
Down the Highway with Edward Abbey   *40*

James R. Hepworth
The Poetry Center Interview   *48*

Nancy Mairs
597ax   *61*

Lawrence Clark Powell
The Angry Lover   *69*

Ron Steffens
Abbey, Edward: Hellraiser 81

Chilton Williamson, Jr.
Abbey Lives! 89

Barry Lopez
Meeting Ed Abbey 96

Richard Shelton
Creeping Up on *Desert Solitaire* 100

James R. Hepworth
Canis Lupus Amorus Lunaticum 117

Dave Solheim and Rob Levin
The *Bloomsbury Review* Interview 138

Robert Houston
Down the River with Edward Abbey 156

Diane Wakoski
Joining the Visionary "Inhumanists" 168

Sam Hamill
Down the River Yin 175

Gary Snyder
A Letter to Ed Abbey 182

Edward Hoagland
Abbey's Road 189

Terry Tempest Williams
A Eulogy for Edward Abbey   *199*

Yves Berger
The Burial of Edward Abbey   *204*

David Petersen
Where Phantoms Come to Brood and Mourn   *211*

Gregory McNamee, Gary Paul Nabhan,
    Ann Zwinger, Peter Warshall, John Nichols,
    Barbara Kingsolver, Kevin Dahl, Bill Hoy,
    R. H. Ring, W. David Laird, Charles Bowden,
    Doug Peacock, and Dave Foreman
Saying Adios to Ed   *223*

C. L. Rawlins
Elegy   *251*

Books by Edward Abbey   *253*

Books About Edward Abbey   *255*

Preface

In Memoriam Edward Abbey, 1927–1989

Edward Abbey, to crib a well-known line from Walt Whitman, contained multitudes. He was a deeply generous man, one of the most generous we have ever known: he was absolutely unsparing of his time, his money, his intelligence, himself. He thrived on thunderous arguments, and, although God knows he could be gruff, he was never discourteous in waging them. He inspired and influenced generations of writers, artists, ecologists, and desert rats, as the contributors to this book attest; almost everyone doing creative work in the American West today owes Ed a debt. He was always sharing some discovery or another, some new novel or painting or essay or mountain trail. He loved good cigars, difficult books of twentieth-century continental philosophy, discussions that went on late into the evening, slow country tunes back-to-back with selections from Brahms and Mozart or from the composer whom he called his hero, Charles Ives. He was fond of thick, grilled, bloody steaks, although he hated the corrupt ranching industry that thrives, subsidized by the American taxpayer, on our public lands. He despised fakery, cowardice, the usual pieties. He applauded deliberation, honorable action, the unfettered mind. He held little sacred, and he vigorously tested the convictions of his friends and opponents alike, probing, questioning, arguing. When he died, on the fourteenth of March, 1989, he left a hole in our hearts, in the heart of the American West, in the heart of modern American writing.

Whatever Ed did, he did with rare good humor, even in the thick of combat; for that reason, he had few real enemies, no matter how controversial the positions he took. When we went together for the first time to Jack's, a now-defunct, chic bar in the heart of downtown Tucson, Ed set the theme by walking through the swinging doors and bellowing, "Smells like lawyers in here!" It was a safe enough accusation, since attorneys are thicker than cockroaches in the booming West; every carefully coiffeured head in the place turned. Ed smiled cordially, flashed that big, toothy, utterly charming grin of his, whereupon all but the most self-important of his targets laughed and settled down to argue politics until closing time. Try Ed's humor for yourself: go out and buy a copy of his novel *The Fool's Progress* (Henry Holt & Co., 1988), published six months before his death to widespread acclaim.

Ed contained multitudes, and he will be remembered in as many ways as there are people who came to know him. One of our favorite reminiscences of Ed comes from a grade-school composition by a young girl named Brady Barnes that Ed showed us one spring day a few years ago. Brady's perceptive, funny account—bearing all the promise of a true writer—delighted him, as he took real joy in so many good and noble things:

FAMOUS STAR EDWARD ABBEY

Edward is a writer. He writes about how to blowup dams. The name of one of the books he wrote was called *Monkey wrench gang*. He wears a black hat with a wrench on it. Ed has

a gray elephant beard and he's a tall, skinny man. Ed does not
like the highway so he throws beer bottles out the window.
Ed does not like t.v. so he took his t.v. outside and took his
gun and shot his t.v. and now it's a sculpture in his backyard.
by Brady.

For our parts, how shall we remember Ed Abbey? First of all,
let us continue to read him, to keep him alive by returning
often to his words. Let us hold *Desert Solitaire* and *The Journey Home* and *Black Sun* and Ed's other books close to our
hearts, recommend them often to others, read them aloud in
lines at the Motor Vehicle Division and the neighborhood
Safeway, talk about them, buy them so that they stay in print
forever. And then, let us continue the struggle to keep something of the real America alive, to preserve the wilderness, to
demand ecological responsibility, to fight for the Earth without compromise: let us act with the courage that Ed taught
us, for he remains among us, a part of the good fight.

Finally, borrowing again from Walt Whitman, let us remember Ed Abbey by honoring a favorite credo:

Resist much, obey little.

RESIST MUCH
OBEY LITTLE

A Few Words in Favor of Edward Abbey

Reading through a sizeable gathering of reviews of Edward Abbey's books, as I have lately done, one becomes increasingly aware of the extent to which this writer is seen as a problem by people who are, or who think they are, on his side. The problem, evidently, is that he will not stay in line. No sooner has a label been stuck to his back by a somewhat hesitant well-wisher than he runs beneath a low limb and scrapes it off. To the consternation of the "committed" reviewer, he is not a conservationist or an environmentalist or a boxable ist of any other kind; he keeps on showing up as Edward Abbey, a horse of another color, and one that requires care to appreciate.

He is a problem, apparently, even to some of his defenders, who have an uncontrollable itch to apologize for him: "Well, he did *say* that. But we mustn't take him altogether seriously. He is only trying to shock us into paying attention." Don't we all remember, from our freshman English class, how important it is to get the reader's attention?

Some environmentalist reviewers see Mr. Abbey as a direct threat to their cause. They see him as embarrassingly prejudiced or radical or unruly. Not a typical review, but representative of a certain kind of feeling about Edward Abbey, was Dennis Drabelle's attack on *Down the River* in *The Nation* of May 1, 1982. Mr. Drabelle accuses Mr. Abbey of elitism, iconoclasm, arrogance, and xenophobia; he finds that Mr. Abbey's "immense popularity among environmentalists is puzzling"; and observes that "many of his attitudes give aid and comfort to the enemies of conservation."

Edward Abbey, of course, is a mortal requiring criticism, and I would not attempt to argue otherwise. He undoubtedly has some of the faults he has been accused of having, and maybe some others that have not been discovered yet. What I *would* argue is that attacks on him such as that of Mr. Drabelle are based on misreading, and that the misreading is based on the assumption that Mr. Abbey is both a lesser man and a lesser writer than he is in fact.

Mr. Drabelle and others like him assume that Mr. Abbey is an environmentalist—hence, that they, as other environmentalists, have a right to expect him to perform as their tool. They further assume that, if he does not so perform, they have a proprietary right to complain. They would like, in effect, to brand him an outcast and an enemy of their movement, and to enforce their judgment against him by warning people away from his books. Why should environmentalists want to read a writer whose immense popularity among them is puzzling?

Such assumptions, I think, rest on yet another that is more important and more needful of attention: the assumption that our environmental problems are the result of bad policies, bad political decisions, and that, therefore, our salvation lies in winning unbelievers to the right political side. If all those assumptions were true, then I suppose that the objections of Mr. Drabelle would be sustainable: Mr. Abbey's obstreperous traits would be as unsuitable in him as in any other political lobbyist. Those assumptions, however, are false.

Mr. Abbey is not an environmentalist. He is, certainly, a defender of some things that environmentalists defend, but he does not write merely in defense of what we call "the environment." Our environmental problems, moreover, are not, at root, political; they are cultural. As Edward Abbey knows and has been telling us, our country is not being destroyed by bad politics; it is being destroyed by a bad way of life. Bad politics is merely another result. To see that the problem is far more than political is to return to reality, and a look at reality permits us to see, for example, what Mr. Abbey's alleged xenophobia amounts to.

The instance of xenophobia cited by Mr. Drabelle occurs on page seventeen of *Down the River*, where Mr. Abbey proposes that our Mexican border should be closed to immigration. If we permit unlimited immigration, he says, before long "the social, political, economic life of the United States will be reduced to the level of life in Juarez, Guadalajara, Mexico City, San Salvador, Haiti, India. To a common peneplain of overcrowding, squalor, misery, oppression, torture, and hate."

That is certainly not a liberal statement. It expresses "contempt for other societies," just as Mr. Drabelle says it does. It is, moreover, a fine example of the exuberantly opinionated Abbey sentence that raises the hackles of readers like Mr. Drabelle—as it is probably intended to do. But before we dismiss it for its tone of "churlish hauteur," we had better ask if there is any truth in it.

And there is some truth in it. As the context plainly shows, this sentence is saying something just as critical of ourselves as of the other countries mentioned. Whatever the justice of the "contempt for other societies," the contempt for the society of the United States, which is made explicit in the next paragraph, is fearfully just: "We are slaves in the sense that we depend for our daily survival upon an expand-or-expire agro-industrial empire—a crackpot machine—that the specialists cannot comprehend and the managers cannot manage. Which is, furthermore, devouring world resources at an exponential rate. We are, most of us, dependent employees."—A statement that is daily verified by the daily news. And its truth exposes the ruthless paradox of Mexican immigration: Mexicans cross the border because our way of life is extravagant; we have no place for them, or won't for very long. A generous immigration policy would be contradicted by our fundamentally ungenerous way of life. Mr. Abbey assumes that, before talking about generosity, we must talk about carrying capacity, and he is correct. The ability to be generous is finally limited by the availability of supplies.

The next question, then, must be: If he is going to write about immigration, why doesn't he do it in a sober, informed, logical manner? The answer, I am afraid, will not suit some advocates of sobriety, information, and logic: He *can* write in a sober, informed, logical manner—if he *wants* to. And why does he sometimes not want to? Because it is not in his character to want to all the time. With Mr. Abbey character is given, or it takes, a certain precedence, and that precedence makes him a writer and a man of a different kind, and probably a better kind, than the practitioner of mere sobriety, information, and logic.

In classifying Mr. Abbey as an environmentalist, Mr. Drabelle is implicitly requiring him to be sober, informed, and logical. And there is nothing illogical about Mr. Drabelle's discomfort when his call for an environmentalist was answered by a man of character, somewhat unruly, who apparently did not know that an environmentalist was expected.

That, I think, is Mr. Abbey's problem with many of his de-
tractors. He is advertised as an environmentalist. They *want*
him to be an environmentalist. And who shows up but this
character, who writes beautifully some of the time, who argues some of the time with great eloquence and power, but
who some of the time offers opinions that appear to be only
his own uncertified prejudices, and who some of the time,
and even in the midst of serious discussion, makes *jokes*.

If Mr. Abbey is not an environmentalist, what is he? He is,
I think, at least in the essays, an autobiographer. He may be
writing on one or another of what are now called environmental issues, but he remains Edward Abbey, speaking as and
for himself, fighting, literally, for dear life. This is important,
for if he is writing as an autobiographer, he *cannot* be writing
as an environmentalist—or as a special ist of any other kind.
As an autobiographer, his work is self-defense. As a conservationist, he is working to conserve himself as a human being. But this is self-defense and self-conservation of the
largest and noblest kind, for Mr. Abbey understands that to
defend and conserve oneself as a human being in the fullest,
truest sense, one must defend and conserve many others and
much else. What would be the hope of being personally
whole in a dismembered society, or personally healthy in a
land scalped, scraped, eroded, and poisoned, or personally
free in a land entirely controlled by the government, or personally enlightened in an age illuminated only by TV? Edward Abbey is fighting on a much broader front than that of
any "movement." He is fighting for the survival, not only of
nature, but of *human* nature, of culture, as only our heritage
of works and hopes can define it. He is, in short, a traditional-
ist—as he has said himself, expecting, perhaps, not to be believed.

Here the example of Thoreau becomes pertinent. My essay may seem on the verge of becoming very conventional now, for one of the strongest of contemporary conventions is that of comparing every writer who has been as far out of the house as the mailbox to Thoreau. But I do not intend to say that Mr. Abbey writes like Thoreau, for I do not think he does, but only that their cases are similar. Thoreau has been adopted by the American environmental movement as a figurehead; he is customarily quoted and invoked as if he were in some simple way a forerunner of environmentalism. This is possible, obviously, only because Thoreau has been dead since 1862. Thoreau was an environmentalist in exactly the same sense that Edward Abbey is: he was for some things that environmentalists are for. And in his own time he was just as much an embarrassment to movements, just as uncongenial to the group spirit, as Edward Abbey is, and for the same reasons: he was working as an autobiographer, and his great effort was to conserve himself as a human being in the best and fullest sense. As a political activist, he was a poor excuse. What was the political value of his forlorn, solitary taxpayer's revolt against the Mexican War? What was politic about his defense of John Brown, or his insistence that abolitionists should free the *wage* slaves of Massachusetts? Who could trust the diplomacy of a man who would pray:

> Great God, I ask thee for no other pelf
> Than that I may not disappoint myself;
>
> And next in value, which thy kindness lends,
> That I may greatly disappoint my friends . . . ?

The point, evidently, is that if we want the human enterprise to be defended, we must reconcile ourselves to the likelihood that it can be defended only by human beings. This, of course, entails an enormous job of criticism: an endless judging and sorting of the qualities of human beings and of their contributions to the human enterprise. But the size and urgency of this job of criticism should warn us to be extremely wary of specializing the grounds of judgment. To judge a book by Edward Abbey by the standard of the immediate political aims of the environmentalist movement is not only grossly unfair to Mr. Abbey, but is a serious disservice to the movement itself.

The trouble, then, with Mr. Abbey—a trouble, I confess, that I am disposed to like—is that he speaks insistently as himself. In any piece of his, we are apt to have to deal with all of him, caprices and prejudices included. He does not simply submit to our criticism, as does any author who publishes, but virtually demands it. And so his defenders, it seems to me, are obliged to take him seriously, to assume that he generally means what he says, and, instead of apologizing for him, to acknowledge that he is not always right or always fair. He is *not*, of course. Who is? For me, part of the experience of reading him has always been, at certain points, that of arguing with him.

My defense of him begins with the fact that I want him to argue with, as I want to argue with Thoreau, another writer full of cranky opinions and strong feelings. If we value these men and their work, we are compelled to acknowledge that such writers are not made by tailoring to the requirements, and trimming to the tastes, of any and all. They submit to standards raised, though not made, by themselves. We, with our standards, must take them as they come, defend ourselves against them if we can, agree with them if we must. If we want to avail ourselves of the considerable usefulness and the considerable pleasure of Edward Abbey, we will have to like him as he is. If we cannot like him as he is, then we will have to ignore him, if we can. My own notion is that he is going to become harder to ignore, and for good reasons—

not the least being that the military-industrial state is working as hard as it can to prove him right.

It seems virtually certain that no reader can read much of Mr. Abbey without finding some insult to something that he or she approves of. Mr. Abbey is very hard, for instance, on "movements"—the more solemn and sacred they are, the more they tempt his ridicule. He is a great irreverencer of sacred cows. There is, I believe, not one sacred cow of the sizeable herd still on the range that he has left ungoosed. He makes his rounds as unerringly as the local artificial inseminator. This is one of his leitmotifs. He gets around to them all. These are glancing blows, mainly, delivered on the run, with a weapon no more lethal than his middle finger. The following is a fairly typical example:

> The essays in *Down the River* are meant to serve as antidotes to despair. Despair leads to boredom, electronic games, computer hacking, poetry and other bad habits.

That example is appropriate here because it passingly gooses one of my own sacred cows: poetry. I am inclined to be tickled rather than bothered by Mr. Abbey's way with consecrated bovines, and this instance does not stop me long. I do pause, nevertheless, to think that *I*, anyhow, would not equate poetry with electronic pastimes. But if one is proposing to take Mr. Abbey seriously, one finally must stop and deal with such matters. Am I, then, a defender of "poetry"? The answer, inevitably, is no; I am a defender of some poems. Any human product or activity that humans defend as a category becomes, by that fact, a sacred cow—in need, by the same fact, of an occasional goosing, and activity, therefore, that arguably serves the public good.

Some instances of this are funnier than others, and readers will certainly disagree as to the funniness of any given instance. But whatever one's opinion, in particular or in general, of Mr. Abbey's blasphemies against sacred cows, one should be wary of the assumption that they are merely humorous, or (as has been suggested) merely "image-making" stunts calculated to sell articles to magazines. They are, I think, gestures or reflexes of his independence—his refusal to speak as a spokesman or a property of any group or movement, however righteous. This keeps the real dimensions and gravity of our problem visible to him, and keeps him from falling for easy answers. You never hear Mr. Abbey proposing that the fulfillment of this or that public program, or the achievement of the aims of this or that movement, or the "liberation" of this or that group will save us. The absence, in him, of such propositions is one of his qualities, and it is a welcome relief.

The funniest and the best of these assaults are the several that are launched head-on against the most exalted of all the modern sacred cows: the self. Mr. Abbey's most endearing virtue as an autobiographer is his ability to stand aside from himself, and recount his most outrageous and self-embarrassing goof-ups, with a bemused and gleeful curiosity, as if they were the accomplishments, not merely of somebody else, but of an altogether different kind of creature. I envy him that. It is, of course, a high accomplishment. How absurd we humans, in fact, are! How misapplied is our self-admiration—as we can readily see by observing other self-admiring humans! How richly just and healthful is self-ridicule! And yet how few of us are capable of it. I certainly do find it hard. My own goof-ups seem to me to have received merciless publicity when my wife has found out about them.

Because he is so humorous and unflinching an autobiographer, he knows better than to be uncritical about anything human. That is why he holds sacred cows in no reverence.

And it is at least partly why his reverence for nature is authentic; he does not go to nature to seek himself or flatter himself, or speak of nature in order to display his sensitivity. He is understandably reluctant to reveal himself as a religious man, but the fact occasionally appears plainly enough: "it seems clear at last that our love for the natural world—Nature—is the only means by which we can requite God's obvious love for it."

The richest brief example of Abbey humor that I remember is his epigram on "gun control" in his essay, "The Right to Arms." "If guns are outlawed," he says, "only the government will have guns." That sentence, of course, is a parody of the "gun lobby" bumpersticker: "If guns are outlawed, only outlaws will have guns." It seems at first only another example of sacred cow goosing—howbeit an unusually clever one, for it gooses both sacred cows involved in this conflict: the idea that, because guns are used in murders, they should be "controlled" by the government, and the idea that the Second Amendment to the Bill of Rights confers a liberty that is merely personal. Mr. Abbey's sentence, masquerading as an instance of his well-known "iconoclasm," slices cleanly through the distractions of the controversy to the historical and constitutional roots of the issue. The sentence is, in fact, an excellent gloss on the word "militia" in the Second Amendment. And so what might appear at first to be merely an "iconoclastic" joke at the expense of two public factions becomes, on examination, the expression of a respectable political fear and an honorable political philosophy, a statement that the authors of our constitution would have recognized and welcomed. The epigram is thus a product of wit of the highest order, richer than the excellent little essay that contains it.

Humor, in Mr. Abbey's work, is a function of his outrage,

and is therefore always answering to necessity. Without his humor, his outrage would be intolerable—as, without his outrage, his humor would often be shallow or self-exploitive. The indispensable work of his humor, as I see it, is that it keeps bringing the whole man into the job of work. Often, the humor is not so much a property of the argument at hand as it is a property of the stance from which the argument issues.

Mr. Abbey writes as a man who has taken a stand. He is an *interested* writer. This exposes him to the charge of being prejudiced, and prejudiced he certainly is. He is prejudiced against tyranny over both humanity and nature. He is prejudiced in favor of democracy and freedom. He is prejudiced in favor of an equitable and settled domestic life. He is prejudiced in favor of the wild creatures and their wild habitats. He is prejudiced in favor of charitable relations between humanity and nature. He has other prejudices too, but I believe that those are the main ones. All of his prejudices, major and minor, identify him as he is, not as any reader would have him be. Because he speaks as himself, he does not represent any group, but he stands for all of us.

He is, I think, one of the great defenders of the idea of property. His novel *Fire on the Mountain* is a moving, eloquent statement on behalf of the personal proprietorship of land—*proper* property. And this espousal of the cause of the private landowners, the small farmers and small ranchers, is evident throughout his work. But his advocacy of that kind of property is balanced by his advocacy of another kind: public property, not as "government land," but as wild land, wild property, which, belonging to nobody, belongs to everybody, including the wild creatures native to it. He understands better than anyone I know the likelihood that one kind of property is not safe without the other. He understands, that is,

the natural enmity between tyranny and wilderness. "Robin
Hood, not King Arthur," he says, "is the real hero of English legend."

You cannot lose your land and remain free; if you keep
your land, you cannot be enslaved. That is an old feeling that
began to work its way toward public principle in our country
at about the time of the Stamp Act. Mr. Abbey inherits it
fully. He understands it both consciously and instinctively. It
is this and not nature love, I think, that is the real motive of
his outrage. His great fear is the fear of dispossession.

But his interest is not just in *landed* property. His enterprise is the defense of all that properly belongs to us,
including all those thoughts and works and hopes that
we inherit from our culture. His work abounds in anti-
intellectual jokes—he is not going to run with *that* pack,
either—but no one can read him attentively without realiz-
ing that he has read well and widely. His love for Bach is virtually a theme of his work. His outrage often vents itself in
outrageousness, and yet it is the outrage of a cultivated
man—that is why it is valuable to us, and why it is interesting.

He is a cultivated man. And he is a splendid writer. Readers who allow themselves to be distracted by his jokes at their
or our or his own expense cheat themselves out of a treasure.
The xenophobic remark that so angers Mr. Drabelle, for example, occurs in an essay, "Down the River with Henry
Thoreau," which is an excellent piece of writing—entertaining, funny some of the time, aboundingly alive and alert, var-
iously interesting, diversely instructive. The river is the
Green, in Utah; the occasion is a boat trip by Mr. Abbey and
five of his friends in November, 1980. During the trip he
read *Walden* for the first time since his school days. This sub-
jection of a human product to "the prehuman sanity of the
desert" is characteristic of Mr. Abbey's work, the result of

one of his soundest instincts. His account of the trip is, at once, a travelogue, a descriptive catalogue of natural sights and wonders, and a literary essay. It is an essay in the pure, literal sense: a trial. Mr. Abbey tries himself against Thoreau and Thoreau against himself; he tries himself and Thoreau against the river; he tries himself and Thoreau and the river against modern times, and vice versa. The essay looks almost capriciously informal; only a highly accomplished and knowledgeable writer would have been capable of it. It is, among all else, a fine literary essay—such a reading of *Walden* as Thoreau would have wanted, not by the faceless automaton of current academic "scholarship," but by a man outdoors, whose character is in every sentence he writes.

I don't know that that essay, good as it is, is outstanding among the many that Mr. Abbey has written. I chose to speak of it because Mr. Drabelle chose to speak of it, and because I think it represents its author well enough. It exhibits one of his paramount virtues as a writer, a virtue paramount in every writer who has it: he is always interesting. I have read, I believe, all of his books except one, and I do not remember being bored by any of them. One reason for this is the great speed and activity of his pages; a page of his, picked at random, is likely, I believe, to have an unusual number of changes of subject, and cover an unusual amount of ground. Another reason is that he does not oversimplify either himself or, despite his predilection for one-liners, his subject. Another reason is his humor, the various forms of which keep breaking through the surface in unexpected places, like wet-weather springs.

But the quality in him that I most prize, the one that removes him from the company of the writers I respect and puts him in the company, the smaller company, of the writers I love, is that he sees the gravity, the great danger, of the predicament we are now in, he tells it unswervingly, and he defends unflinchingly the heritage and the qualities that may preserve us. I read him, that is to say, for consolation, for the comfort of being told the truth. There is no longer any honest way to deny that a way of living that our leaders continue to praise is destroying all that our country is and all the best that it means. We are living even now among punishments and ruins. For those who know this, Edward Abbey's books will remain an indispensable solace. His essays, and his novels too, are "antidotes to despair." For those who think that a few more laws will enable us to go on safely as we are going, Abbey's books will remain—and good for him!—a pain in the neck.

A Note on Ed Abbey

I first met Ed Abbey at my ranch in Cuba, New Mexico. I taught Ed how to ride and punch cattle. When the cattle started to punch back, Ed decided to become a writer. Ed discovered that to become a writer you must learn to drink a lot, which can be accomplished with much practice and dedication to the art. The art of drinking. What tempted Ed into the writing trade was what got the best of us into it. You can sleep late. Those who take writing seriously solemnly end up in Hollywood writing "The Guiding Light" and "Little House on the Prairie."

Ed decided early in life to save the planet, and he damn near did. First of all you have to learn to write well—which Ed did—then you have to bum around the country to discover who's going to blow us up—which Ed did. Then Ed set about blowing them up—and he did.

I went on one expedition with Ed outside Flagstaff while Ed was working at Sunset Crater, and we carved down a huge Las Vegas girlie sign that was hiding the West. I can't say this is true, because that is illegal, but someone did it while we were in that area. Some bad people carved down all the expensive signs between Albuquerque and Santa Fe. I can't say we had anything to do with it, because such an act would be attacking the free-enterprise system. Ed would never attack the free-enterprise system that hides the West. He would never work against the game-of-grab system that rewarded him so generously. Ed called me to ask whether he should accept a tiny offer from a movie company to buy *The Brave Cowboy*. I told him it would probably have to be that small sum—or *nada*. Ed was broke when they paid a Hollywood scriptwriter a fortune and shot the film outside of Albuquerque and generously gave Ed a job as an extra. After that, Ed would never think of attacking the great American system that is dedicated to helping the struggling artist.

Ed was fortunate in his wandering to pick up some attractive characters such as Doug Peacock, who chose to live with a bunch of grizzly bears in Glacier Park and make his fight with them against the deadly white man. I recognize many of Ed's characters from real life whom he has, with his talent, made into alive-on-the-page people.

Ed, like the rest of us here in the boondocks, has not had much luck with the effete Eastern gang that controls the critics' pages. Ed frightens the critics. Ed does not fit into their charming literary world. Ed doesn't use big enough words. Worst of all, he wants to write about what's happening in America outside the suburbs of New York.

The New York publishers are cooperating with the Eastern gang and are careful not to overadvertise Ed's books, as though they don't want to be caught peddling such offensive writing that threatens the establishment, that threatens the conglomerate monopoly those publishers have become.

Why can't Mister Abbey write books that show the true beauty and the true manliness of the progressive spirit of the West? After all, Zane Grey and our own Louis L'Amour sell millions of copies of awesome literature that Duke Wayne would be proud to place on the silver screen. Can fifty million readers be wrong? Instead of writing about the picturesque characters that populate the colorful West, why does Mister Abbey continuously harp on the bulldozer burial of the West? Why does Mister Abbey attack the Park Service and the Forest Service that gave him the jobs that allowed him to write his books? You'd think Mister Abbey would appreciate a system that gave him the inside knowledge and the weapons to expose the big scam.

I visited Ed many times high in his swaying towers overlooking what's left of the National Forests. Ed scribbling away, trying to rescue the beauty that remains. We could see the plume from the distant smelter that formed black dollar signs as it wept its way toward the last of the West, sprinkling its acid rain as it went. Who cares? Just a few: Ed Abbey and his Monkey Wrench Gang. The kind of people who should be deported. Sent back to where they came from.

Ed came from a small town in Pennsylvania called Home. Since I've known Ed he has been threatening to write about his hobo-like picaresque adventures in the rambling trade since leaving Home. I hope that's the book he tells me he is now on Page 900 of. If so, Thomas Wolfe was wrong. You can go home again. At least we can find out what happened to one of this country's best writers since he quit a place by that name. As Casey Stengel, that great Brooklyn Dodger philosopher, said in Stengelese, "I don't make predictions, especially about the future." Nevertheless, I hope the future weather charts predict less acid rain and more Edward Abbey.

Scarlet "A" on a Field of Black

I.

Sunrise in Tucson, Arizona, red and purer than the dawn in Erewhon.

An incendiary light hugs the Santa Catalina Mountains, showers down on the survey stakes and luxury-condominium developments littering the pockmarked hillsides, and comes to rest on the reddish-gray bajada of the north slope, hard by the state prison farm. Cactus wrens, mockingbirds, and palomitas vie to make the loudest call over the thunder of sonic booms. Roadrunners peck at roadkills. A handful of desert bighorn, one of hundreds of endangered species inhabiting this place, scramble about the talus scatters. Below them electrified fences ringing intercontinental-missile silos glitter in the growing heat and intensity of light.

It is a typical Western town: slow, mean-spirited, xenophobic, pious, full of realtors, self-ordained ministers of crystal-worshipping pseudoreligions, bad artists, developers. Its transplanted economy is equally typical of the new American West: cattle, agribusiness, "clean" industry, some reclamation project or another, absentee landlordism. It is a place of failed dreams and tired acclimation to things as they are. A town full of the wrong kind of people in public office, the wrong kind of people in the welfare line, Tucson is a metaphor for something much larger.

This is Edward Abbey's home. It is an appropriate, if ironic setting: everything he hates and everything he loves converge and await together Abbey's first bleary uncoffeed gaze at the new morning. Murderousness, greed, and rapacity on the one hand; beauty, light, and the serenity of the desert on the other. And in between a truckstop or two and a banner, black, emblazoned with a monkey wrench.

Edward Abbey need not stray far from home to find an abundance of targets for his ready pen. What he requires to flesh out the subplot of a novel or the farther paragraphs of a political manifesto stands everywhere before him. Throw a rock from Abbey's study into the boomtown desert and, more often than not, you'll peg a cryptofascist, a snakeoil peddler, a land-rapist, a fundamentalist, a drifter out for a fast buck. The range of evils in boomtown Tucson is vast and seemingly endless—but not necessarily inescapable. Which is, I suppose, why Abbey likes it here.

II.

All machines have their friction. But when the friction comes to
have its machine, and oppression and robbery are organized,
I say, let us not have such a machine any longer.
Henry David Thoreau, 1849

Art cannot be separated from politics. The opinion that it can be, George Orwell reminds us, in itself constitutes a political position. Edward Abbey's writing cannot be fully understood without recognizing that a profound, little-known political conviction underlies and motivates it. To dispense with labels from the outset: in the realm of ideal politics, Edward Abbey is an anarchist.

The issue is not artificial. It arises because Abbey urges it to arise. For Abbey's books, from *Jonathan Troy* to *The Fool's Progress*, are communiques straight from the war zone—grown hopelessly close now—where the State opposes the individual, where the collectivist tendencies of modern nations, themselves becoming more and more alike, conspire to crush those who wish to be left in peace.

The very term *anarchism* forces battle. Thanks to the mad French cafe bomber Ravachol and the inductive distortions of the propagandists who made of him a cause célèbre, the term conjures up a vision of deviance in the popular imagination. Endomorphic psychopaths mow down the innocent and the guilty alike with a crazed chuckle and a hot pipe-bomb; drunken proletarian mobs massacre priests on the altar and cart off the possessions of the hardworking middle class; blood flows in the gutter. Those whom anarchism would displace keep such images current, essential to the popular definition of a political creed that means, at heart, "no rulers," not "no rule."

Abbey's anarchism departs from the vulgar characterizations spawned by our media, our educators, our government. His anarchism is a positive force proclaiming the individual as the basis of civil society and trade. It is, he has written, nothing more than "democracy taken seriously." It holds that the one social necessity is absolute liberty for all. It recognizes but one law: no person may aggress against another. It argues that governments are evil by their nature, committing mass murder in the form of war, theft in the form of taxation. Because of the fundamentally antisocial character of the State, all governments, this anarchism maintains, must be abolished.

Edward Abbey's work, taken as a whole, can be seen as an unwavering meditation on that uncomplicated moral and political theory, one that proclaims its essence in Abbey's elegant formulation, "the root of all evil is the love of power." *The Monkey Wrench Gang*, his best-known novel, is an ode to individual liberty and the preservationist ethic of saving the land from a cancerous machine. *The Brave Cowboy* and *Good News* are thinly veiled exhortations to resist tyranny wherever it is met, by whatever means necessary. *Desert Solitaire* is a manifesto of the unchained soul, an inspired argument that human beings, like ecosystems, fare best when left alone. In Abbey's universe, art and politics are inseparable. In his words, "it is the writer's duty to hate injustice, to defy the powerful, and to speak for the voiceless." His writing is a call to arms.

III.

If you understand your true mission and the very interests of art itself, come with us. Place your pen, your pencil, your chisel, your ideas at the service of the revolution. *Peter Kropotkin, 1880*

You cannot be free in a dying land if you lack the will to fight for its life—or to move on to fight elsewhere. You will not save the world or even a small corner of your soul through drunken, meaningless peroration to no one in particular. So Abbey posits in *Jonathan Troy*, his first novel, published in 1959, when he was thirty-two years old.

When the police have all manner of air cover and firepower and your spirit cannot brook jails or metropolises, strike out on your own for the wilderness, like the brave cowboy in Abbey's book of that name, where, if nothing else, you can establish "bases for guerrilla warfare against tyranny," as did the Monkey Wrench Gang.

When your rights are abrogated by the State and its hired guns there is but one thing to do: resist, even if resistance means your death. So Abbey, through John Vogelin, the hero of *Fire on the Mountain*.

Resist much, obey little.

Many other writers have said as much, among them Henry David Thoreau and Walt Whitman, but Abbey's pronouncements acquire a peculiar force today simply by virtue of their outlandishness. No one else is making them, at least through the vehicle of popular literature. The smart money among modern American writers is instead on tales of suburban passion, middle-aged angst, campus adultery, space rockets, and demonically possessed Chryslers. It is not on telling readers, whom it is assumed should not be unduly challenged by ideas, that unless they shape up and begin to take responsibility for their own lives, they're going to wake up one morning to a ruined Earth and the crunch of truncheons—delivered with a California stylishness—slaves to a new order of machines and might. For all that's said and taught about the restorative and revolutionary power of words, few contemporary writers concern themselves with questions of social need and clear and present dangers to our liberty. For most, the audience is the narcoleptic and the voyeur, the future a shopping spree. Their duty, it seems, is less to their future than to their bankroll.

So if Edward Abbey writes with the distance of a prophetic voice crying in the wilderness, *vox clamantis in deserto*, it is simply because he has so little immediate company. Would that it were not so.

IV.

Civilization is a youth with a Molotov cocktail in his hand;
culture is the Soviet tank or the L.A. cop that guns him down.
Edward Abbey, 1968

Where the realm of ideal politics and that of the "real world"—as self-styled pragmatists and apologists for things as they are like to call it—coincide, one learns to expect paradoxes. The range of human possibilities, after all, is cast in relative terms; no party lines exist in nature (the claims of sociobiology notwithstanding); black and white bound a multitude of colors. Which is by way of prelude to saying that Edward Abbey's books, despite their informed political vision, are not the place to go for a systematic, uncompromised philosophy of modern anarchism, where all ends well and all contradictions melt into air, resolved by a handy syllogism and a deft stroke of the pen. For that we have William Godwin, whose *Enquiry Concerning Political Justice* (1793) prefigures John Vogelin's stand in *Fire on the Mountain*. We have Pierre-Joseph Proudhon, whose *Qu'est-ce que la Propriété* (1840) can be read as the first plank of the preservationism Abbey has espoused in many speeches and essays. We have Peter Kropotkin, whose marvelous *Memoirs of a Revolutionist* (1899) recounts a flight from the oppressive city echoed years later by Will Gatlin of *Black Sun*.

Abbey is an artist, not a systematist; a novelist, not a prophet. (Many of his readers, it seems, overlook these nice distinctions.) Only once did he attempt to construct a formal theoretical framework to justify his political positions, and that was long ago, and in another land: in 1959, when Abbey submitted to his graduate committee at the University of New Mexico a manuscript of some one hundred pages' extent to satisfy the requirement for the master's degree in philosophy. Entitled "Anarchism and the Morality of Violence," the unpublished manuscript comprises Abbey's exploration of the philosophical bases underlying anarchist theory and their relationship to the practicalities of making a revolution. Is the act of assassination, Abbey asks at the outset, morally justifiable? Abbey never tells us—after all, this is a school thesis, a form inhospitable to original thought in the place of received wisdom and surveys of the literature. Instead, he weighs the formulations of the great anarchist philosophers—Godwin, Proudhon, Bakunin, Kropotkin, and Sorel—to arrive at an academically defensible conclusion: assassination and other acts of political violence *may* be excused under a strict set of morally derived criteria, but they are never desirable. So much for Ravachol and Leon Czolgosz.

Abbey still holds to this view; it is mirrored in his fiction, as it is in his brief 1987 essay "Theory of Anarchy," written for the radical environmental journal *Earth First!* The Monkey Wrench Gang, like the real-life ecoanarchists Abbey has inspired, is made up not of terrorists but saboteurs, latter-day Luddites who destroy machines instead of people, the exact counter to the practices of modern government. (Remember Jimmy Carter's neutron bomb.) In Abbey's work, no protagonist initiates acts of force, of violence against others. The only moral justification for violent acts—as in *The Monkey Wrench Gang* and *Good News*—is self-defense. It is not John Vogelin who brings warfare into the craggy mountains of western New Mexico, not George Hayduke who fires from a multimillion-dollar helicopter gunship. That great symbol, the monkey wrench, is a tool made to be used on other tools, and not, like the billyclub, on people's heads. And it was not

Edward Abbey who first came up with the notion of surgically bombing nonmilitary targets.

Violence is abhorrent, but it must remain an option in Abbey's world, fictional and real. That is the first paradox. How can the polarization necessary to a popular uprising against government be introduced without acts of force? How can one argue for civil war and at the same time maintain that political violence is ultimately unjustifiable?

There are no easy answers, surely none from Abbey himself. But there will be ample time and need to think of them, should Abbey's vision of the probable future be realized.

V.

What reason have we Americans to think that our own society
will necessarily escape the world-wide drift toward the
totalitarian organization of men and institutions?
Edward Abbey, 1968

Recognize paradox, for it is your daily companion. There are no ready answers, no panaceas; perhaps there is not even hope. Make a stand and sooner or later you'll find yourself straddling a faultline—which is fine by Abbey.

Consider preservationism, for instance. Abbey often deals with this large issue, one that should be vital to modern anarchist theory. Preservationism—or "deep ecology," as it is sometimes known—calls for a fundamental revaluation of our attitudes toward the hierarchies of nature, of our place in the global ecosystem. It calls for humans to recognize themselves not as masters but as wards and caretakers of the planet. Preservationism demands the end of human government of wild lands and undomesticated species—the tamed world already being, it is feared, a total loss. In other words, preservationism is an ill-defined but universal anarchism taken beyond the purely social level. As the ecologist and writer Gary Paul Nabhan put it, "we must learn that we are but one of forty thousand vertebrate species and act accordingly."

Because a unified theory of preservationism has not been clearly set out, owing to the fearful tendency of leftists to tear apart organized approaches to anything, many questions go unanswered. In a stateless society, how are common lands and resources to be used? How are boundaries between the wild and the domesticated worlds to be determined? How are lands to be maintained and conserved? How shall humans obtain what they need? Who will decide? Within Abbey's preservationist ethic lies a tangle of dilemmas, and few hard answers—and, regrettably, few hard thoughts from other anarchists.

Under the slash-and-burn junta of Ronald Reagan, environmental theory has had increasingly to grapple with just such questions. As a result, it has polarized into two camps: those who would exploit all available resources, no matter where they might lie—public lands and legacies be damned —and those who, like Abbey, maintain that the only possible position to take on wilderness is to leave it alone, period. Throughout the Reagan years, thanks to James Watt, Donald Hodel, and other adherents to the clearcut and bulldoze school, the first position, however, gained the field, driven by mindless appeals to national security and blind patriotism: Do you want to see the nation sold down the river, after all, to the Saudis and the Japanese? Then let's rip apart the Rocky Mountains for shale oil right quick.

The Reaganite approach to wilderness has led the field

only, it appears, because so few of Edward Abbey's fellow citizens are troubled by the prospect of a wilderness-free nation, so long as their resource needs—most of them not "needs" at all—are met, so long as their dependence can masquerade as the exercise of freedom of choice. There are still more recreational vehicles than environmentalists. Since anarchism, under which preservationism may one day be subsumed, is ideally the one truly democratic political ideology (no power for all), what can one do with the horrible impression that the polity would just as soon see a Disneyland built midway down the Grand Canyon as save Rainbow Bridge from further destruction or the continental shelf from offshore drilling? The paradox again.

Of course, Abbey's argument for wilderness preservation, outlined in *Desert Solitaire* and elsewhere, neatly sidesteps issues of aesthetics and the public good. His is romantic. We need wilderness, he says, not to inspire benevolence in our hearts but to stage wars of resistance when the going gets really bad, a point well understood by Fidel Castro, Mao, and Robert E. Lee. Whatever the case, Abbey has not proposed any real solution to the perfidious relationship between his countrymen and the land. He has instead gone in for skirmishing, as, for instance, when in recent years he has urged that cattle—hooved locusts, as he calls them—be removed from public lands throughout the American West, leading to a new range war, with ranchers everywhere howling for his blood.

Or consider immigration, on which Abbey's position has earned him even greater than his usual notoriety, at first in southern Arizona, and then nationwide. Abbey fired his opening shot in a letter to the *New York Review of Books* of December 17, 1981, in which, arguing from the "overcrowded lifeboat" theory, he called for an immediate halt to immigration into America, especially from Mexico and Central America. Abbey proposed that the current United States Border Patrol be expanded to a force of at least twenty thousand heavily armed guards, so that the American way of life might be made safe from the Mexican threat "to degrade and cheapen [it] downward to the Hispanic standard."

Here the paradox arises ugly and mean. Anarchism, recognizing no government, acknowledges no nation-state, and therefore no national borders. It further advances the right of freedom of movement and of self-determination. Anarchism—and, by extension, the practical anarchist—would cut its own throat were it to call in whatever way for increased State police power. Never mind the uncomfortable overtones of racial superiority, for which anarchism can find no room, and which Abbey has yet to disavow.

In a series of letters to southern Arizona newspapers, Abbey later suggested that what he really wanted was for the Border Patrol to issue rifles and ammunition, gratis, to Mexican would-be immigrants at the border and to point them southward to Mexico City, where they might complete the aborted revolution begun seventy-five years earlier. The next several years saw Abbey further elaborating this argument, gleefully urging that the tide of immigrants from Latin America be turned away at the American frontier, while leftists, liberals, businesspeople, Mexican American groups, conservatives, and Western congressmen joined battle against him in growing numbers. For all this, and perhaps because of the controversy he has inspired, Abbey remains a keen supporter of the closed border, writing letter after angry letter in support of the cause to anyone who might print them.

The paradoxical confluence of the real and the ideal.

What else can one do but recognize it? After all, it has us hard by the throat, and it shows no sign of ever relaxing its grip. But to recognize it is not to become its slave.

VI.

Do I advocate another revolution? What do you mean, *another?* We have yet to see the first. But it's coming.   *Edward Abbey, 1979*

Tucson, Arizona. Edward Abbey's front yard.

Not Edward Abbey's American West, though. Not the West of free rivers, unexplored mountain ranges, virgin forests, and open grasslands, but that of Glen Canyon Dam, the Central Utah Project, strip mines, clearcut hillsides, Los Angeles, and a dozen more unsightly megalopolises. Not wilderness but human savagery. Not packmules but bulldozers. A West bristling with enemies—corporate capitalism, utilities, the Army Corps of Engineers, the Bureau of Land Management and the quisling Environmental Protection Agency, nuclear physicists, politicians, car dealers, developers—and without enough friends.

Things are pretty bad out here. There is no time left for writing to senators or for praying for the redemption of our souls. Things are bad. They're getting worse.

All this is a given. Because of the unabating rape of our land, because we are fast losing our American citizenship to that of violent new Sparta, if his past performance is a reliable guide, then Edward Abbey's politics and writing can become only angrier, more apocalyptic. The Western states, long accustomed to economic and political vassalage to Eastern capital, but also to a certain freedom hard to find elsewhere, are fast discovering that there is no longer room for the individual direction of a John Vogelin, the anarchic vision of an Edward Abbey.

That is why Abbey raises the black flag. That is why he writes: so that, in his words, "the fires of revolt may be kindled—which means hope for us all." Hope that some day we might live in a society of free men and women, tied responsibly and voluntarily to one another and to the Earth. Hope that we can put aside our violence and petty viciousness. Above all, hope that we can find it in ourselves to change the world.

Edward Abbey, Anarchism, and the Environment

One time, Ed Abbey and I were talking about an upcoming election. Ed said to me, "I'm a registered anarchist."

I asked him, "How long have you been a registered anarchist?"

Ed said, "Oh, about 5,000 years. In the realm of ideal politics, I'm some sort of agrarian, barefoot wilderness eco-freak anarchist. One of my favorite thinkers is Prince Kropotkin. Another is Henry Thoreau."

Professionally, Abbey's greatest wish was to be regarded as a fine writer, a literary man. Many's the time Abbey confided that he felt that New York publishers thought he'd been born on the wrong side of the Hudson. But after due consideration, he concluded that the wrong side was actually the right side—and that New York writers were a boring lot, in the main. Most of them were "toadies" and "sycophants," "brown-nosers" and "ass-kissers." What most of them write about has little to do with reality. Rather, they spread a patina of anthropomorphism across the fabric of their lives in the dim hope that something might register as meaningful. Sez Ed, "How can you get excited about someone named Rabbit, for Chrissake?"

Good question.

A major principle of Edward Abbey's character was to *follow the truth no matter where it leads*. This has to be a part of the long-term Abbey heritage. I know this was inherent in both his parents. His father, who passed away earlier this year [1992], had been something of a political iconoclast in his youth, proud of having met Eugene Debs, a quoter of Walt Whitman, and a crack shot to boot. He was a Pennsylvania woodcutter still active with his axe and saw four months before he died at the age of ninety-one. He was self-sufficient and self-directed and he influenced Abbey enormously.

Abbey's mother was a tiny lady, sharp of wit, a fine musician, and a talented writer whose journals revealed that her son, Ned, as he was known, had already turned cantankerous at the age of four years!!

Ed Abbey was my best friend, *el compañero de mi vida*. We went on dozens of camping trips together and hiked thousands of miles carrying on a conversation that lasted for decades. We kept no secrets from each other and we talked about anything and everything that either of us could think of. After four of us carried him deep into the wilderness desert to bury him, there was plenty of time to ruminate on the nature of my friend, and the meaning of his life.

Nearly two years after his death, Michael Pietsch, then at Crown Publishers, asked me if I would be interested in doing a book about Ed. At first I didn't want to. Ed was my friend, not a subject for a book by me. But I remembered that on at least three occasions Ed had suggested that I be his "chronicler," as he put it. Since 1982, he and I both knew the odds favored my outlasting him. It was that summer that he keeled over in my living room and the doctors who treated him at the hospital in Santa Fe erroneously told him he would die in

two months. Ed turned to me and said, "At least I don't have
to floss anymore."

So I agreed to write his biography. In order to do a proper
job of it, I've tried my best to remember all of our conversations together. I've reread all of Ed's books and pored over
his journals, prying as deep into his mind as I can. I spent
Ed's sixty-second birthday with him in Tucson. He told me
then, as he had on the previous Thanksgiving and Christ-
mas, that he wasn't going to last much longer. His greatest
hope was that he could finish writing *Hayduke Lives!* before
he died. He loaded me up with his books, making sure that I
had extra copies of everything he had written. We were doing our level best to be honest with each other, but we had
our own myths to live out. I remember as we walked from his
writing cabin back up to his house I said, "Ed, we still have
another thousand campfires together."

He said, "You're goddam right, *frijol viejo.*"

Ed died six weeks later.

So now I'm 155,000 words into a book that feels like it's
being ghost-edited by Abbey. I'll say this. I accept full responsibility for all of its flaws. After all, it's my fingers that
are pushing down the keys on the keyboard. But the spirit of
this book is definitely in keeping with the spirit of my *compañero.*

Ed was the most consistent person I've ever known. Even
his handwriting remained essentially the same from the time
he was nineteen onward. I have a letter he wrote to his
mother in his own hand when he was an MP in Italy back in
1946 which corroborates this.

Abbey was consistent but he was also extremely complex.
While I can mention some of his outstanding characteristics,
I have to say that he was infinitely greater than the sum of
these characteristics. He was a real man of flesh and blood

subject to the same array of emotions and biases as any other human. He has to be perceived within the context of his milieu. He felt that he had been born either fifty years too late or a hundred years too soon. His widow, my dear friend Clarke Abbey, said that he was born at exactly the right time, that who would he have been without his cause? I say that no matter when he had been born, he would have emerged as a powerful voice in behalf of justice. There are those who feel that Edward Abbey was a great man. I knew him as well as anyone, and I would agree.

His intellect was enormous. He read incessantly and well and was able to quote major passages that had caught his fancy. Many a time when we went camping, we would each take a few books, making sure that we weren't duplicating anything. We would both read in the afternoons when the sun was high. Usually by the end of a camping trip, Ed would have read all of the books that we had both brought. If there was a book that he regarded particularly highly, he would buy me a copy of the same edition so that we could discuss it. He added dozens of books to my library including works by Lucretius, Schopenhauer, Woodcock, Eastlake, McGuane, Harrison, Celine, McCarthy, Thoreau, Hardin, and Whitman. He had read all the major and many of the minor Western philosophers. He devoured good fiction. I remember one time he had come to help my wife and me build our house. We were camped under a juniper tree and Ed was reading Pynchon's *Gravity's Rainbow* by kerosene lamp as we three crowded under a lean-to trying to stay dry that rainy summer night in 1973. Abruptly, Ed snapped the book shut and said, "There. I finished it. Someone had to do it. Now you do it." He handed me the book, rolled over in his sleeping bag and went to sleep.

Abbey had an enormous appreciation of music that lasted

his entire life. His mother was a keyboard player and many a night Ed and his siblings fell asleep listening to her playing. He strongly considered devoting his life to musical composition rather than writing literature. He had a huge collection of long-playing records that featured composers from the Baroque period to the present. It must have been around 1970 and Ed was still living in the rock house in Sabino Canyon. I had gone to visit him. I was sleeping in my truck in front of his house. Sometime before dawn, Ed stealthily carried a speaker out and mounted it just beyond the open window of my camper. Then, just before the sun came up, Ed turned on his phonograph player full blast and I was suddenly listening to a Beethoven symphony. Ed came rushing out of the house with a big grin, looking anxiously at me. "What in the hell are you doing?" I asked. "I just wanted to see what you looked like waking up to Beethoven," he said.

Abbey loved women. He regarded his desire to make love to many women as a biological imperative that has absolutely nothing to do with chauvinism. A billennia of monkey genes do not a monogam make. When he was younger, he seriously considered himself to be victimized by satyrmania. He was married five times, divorced thrice, widowed once, and was finally reshaped by his commitment to his last wife for whom he proved to be a good husband.

Abbey believed in friendship. To him this was sacred. He was as loyal a friend as one could ever have. When he was a student recipient of a Fulbright scholarship in Edinburgh, Scotland, in 1951, he wrote the following: "God help me, I will never sacrifice a friend to an ideal. I will never betray a friend for the sake of any cause. I will never reject a friend in order to stand by an institution. Great nations may fall in dusty ruin before I will sell a friend to save them. I pray to the god within me to give me the power to live by this design."

This appeal was central to one of Abbey's finest novels, *The Brave Cowboy*. Being a true friend was fundamental to Abbey's nature and hearkens back to a time when a man's word was inviolate, when an agreement between men was sealed with a clasp of the hand.

Abbey was a true anarchist. It was not a subject to which he paid lip service. He was the real McCoy. When he was a graduate student at the University of New Mexico back in the '50s, he wrote his master's thesis which was entitled, "Anarchism and the Morality of Violence." It focused on the works of Proudhon, Sorel, Godwin, Bakunin, and Kropotkin. In his journal, Ed wrote, "My favorite melodramatic theme is of the harried anarchist, a wounded wolf, struggling toward the green hills, or the black-white alpine mountains, or the purple-golden desert range, and liberty. Will he make it? Or will the FBI shoot him down on the very threshold of wilderness and freedom? Obviously."

Variations on this theme prevailed in most of Abbey's eight novels. He was convinced that "Government derives its moral authority from those whose ends it serves." He fully realized that "his own liberty was to a high degree dependent upon respecting the rights of others, thus limiting his own liberty in order to secure and increase it." For years, it was Abbey's great fantasy that a small group of families comprised of trusted friends who were creative and committed to wilderness preservation should buy land together and thus found an anarchist commune which would be governed by consensus and NOT laws. Ed had a hell of a time even identifying three or four other true anarchists, let alone getting us to agree where to buy land. Together, Abbey and I looked at land from the Henry Mountains to the Sonoran Desert to the Chihuahuan Desert to the high country of northern New Mexico. We came close a couple of times for we dearly wanted to be neighbors. But we never did buy land together.

Then there was the anarchist adobe houseboat. If ever there was a symbol of absolute evil in Ed's mind it was the Glen Canyon Dam that plugs the once mighty Colorado River. We would build an adobe houseboat, fill it with high explosives, sink it just upstream from the damn dam after having pre-set a triggering device, and watch it blow the dam to smithereens, our rubber rafts ready to catch the crest of the first wave and take what was sure to be the swiftest, most exciting trip down Grand Canyon any boatman has ever had!

Abbey loved the natural world, or wilderness. He loved it for its own sake. His refined sense of egalitarianism extended far beyond the realm of man to include all species of fauna *and* flora, and even beyond that to include the rocks, the air, the water. He perceived everything to be part of a whole.

The adventurer in Abbey required wilderness in order to become a part of it. Wilderness challenged Ed, but not in the sense that one would defeat the other. Rather, there ensued a collaboration between Ed and wilderness that would profoundly affect environmentalist thinking by the final decades of the twentieth century. Ed would disappear into the desert, or deep into a canyon, or up a mountain, or down a river. There he would open himself to the flow of Nature and absorb its message. In *Desert Solitaire* he wrote, "I dream of a hard and brutal mysticism in which the naked self merges with a non-human world and somehow survives still intact, individual, separate." He spent many years of his life as a back-country ranger or fire lookout, always ranging, always looking. He loved wilderness with a total and abiding love that was fired by an enormous, powerful passion. He came to fully realize that as wilderness is reduced by the hand of man in his personal or corporate greed, biotic diversity is threatened, reduced—and that Nature is seen simplistically as a reservoir of natural resources and not what it really is—a planetary biotic community of which humanity is simply a single species, a member species, perhaps a species which has worn out its welcome!

As Ed would withdraw from wilderness solitude profoundly refreshed in spirit, his anger at human encroachment grew. His anarchist tendencies matured. His love of wilderness and his sense of anarchism melded into a single, complex fundament of his being. Through his great talent for writing, he himself became a vehicle and launched a relentless attack against those who would inordinately prosper at the expense of wilderness. He attacked developers who would claim the land and then sell the land for profit. He attacked extractors of natural resources who left in their wake mountains of overburden, thousands of roads, polluting poisons, and general devastation. He attacked public land ranchers whose cattle steal habitat from wildlife. He attacked government agencies including the Bureau of Reclamation for damming, condemning wild rivers; the BLM whom he regarded as the Bureau of Livestock and Mining; the Animal Damage Control who kill—*murder*—predatory wildlife in the erroneous belief that the lifestyle of a rancher is worth more than the life of a mountain lion. He attacked the entire panoply of bureaucracies which he was convinced had driven American society over the edge of ruin.

Now that Ed lies far beyond the reach of the statute of limitations, it can be revealed that he did *not* limit his attacks against wilderness rapists to his writings. He was an activist, a warrior armed with the tools of a warrior. With firearms, flammables, wit, and courage, he physically destroyed those metal marauders that raze wilderness. He pulled up stakes. He closed roads. He did everything he could think of to thwart the juggernaut of so-called human progress *save one thing*—he never, ever caused harm to another human being. However, he did tell me that he could easily foresee a time when even that terrible situation might arise—a time when the government would so impose a police state on what remains of wildlife habitat, that battles would rage between man and man. But by then it would already be too late and the only spoils of such a conflict would be principles.

Edward Abbey has thus far inspired two generations of environmentalists to seek means of decentralizing control of the land. He has inspired people to think of the land in terms of ecosystems, not geopolitical systems.

It is my opinion that Edward Abbey's greatest single contribution to Western culture has been to meld environmentalism and anarchism. Abbey has inspired a coterie of discerning, stout-hearted, wilderness-loving *thinkers* to fully understand that, *"A patriot must always be ready to defend his country against his government."*

Down the Highway
with Edward Abbey

I'm driving Ed Abbey's Cadillac to Denver. It has moldered away in a dirt alley off Tucson's venerable main drag, and now it's going to reside in a pricey Republican enclave on the compromised high plains outside the mile-high city. Of course, if I told you which 'burb it was, I'd have to kill you.

A fire-engine red '75 Eldorado, it has been parked for a year behind Ed's pal Buffalo Medicine's house, accumulating a thick coat of dust and a calligraphy of cat and raccoon tracks across its massive hood. The cables have fallen loose in the engine compartment, the generator's shot, weeds have choked the wheels, and the ragtop's in sad shape. Local writers cruise by occasionally, tip their gimme caps, raise a can of Coors, and drive away. Their wheels churn up the alley dirt, adding another layer of dust to the Caddie. Just like Ed's memory.

Buffalo Medicine has possibly rooked El Piloto, a devotee of the Abbeyite Order, by selling him the car for money which might or might not be too much. Opinions vary. It all depends on where you're positioned in the continuing Ed debate. In Tucson, the debate is quite personal, since locals trade Ed-sightings like baseball cards.

Ed Abbey—Sasquatch.

Along with the Ed-sightings, we are confronted with the most peculiar facet of the Dead-Ed Industry, the I-Was-Ed-Abbey's-Best-Friend Industry. Outside of Tucson, it's moderated a bit by distance into the I-Was-Ed-Abbey's-Biggest-Fan Industry. Shady dudes who may have tipped back a Dos Equis with Ed at a barbecue will now offer you insights into his soul, and a few of these Best Friends will offer to take Biggest Fans to Ed's "secret" gravesite where more Dos Equis can be consumed. Of course, East Coast tenderfoots could be led to my back yard and told the mulch pile is Ed's grave, and they'd go home happy. I wonder how many people have stared at a thoroughly empty pile of dirt in Saguaro National Monument and said perfectly lovely things—into thin air. Nobody seems to find this behavior creepy.

It is a telling measure of the man, and all he accomplished, that so many are willing to define themselves by proximity—real or imagined—to his being.

How much would you pay for a piece of Ed Abbey? We are in a dicey period here, where shit-heads Ed wouldn't have spit on if they were burning buy his books and seven Earth First! T-shirts and claim to be his soul mates. But El Piloto, possibly as thorny and ultimately as sentimental a man as Ed, has bought the car for Love. I wonder what he'll do when the Dead-Ed Industry washes a bibliophile to his door with a limp check for $28,000, dying to drive a piece of the myth.

What can I say? I stole Ed's pencil out of the car and am hiding it in my office. That's a writer for you: happy hypocrites.

One thing's for sure: Rudolfo A. Anaya won't be offering anybody money for Ed's chariot. When he heard El Piloto and I were motoring cross-country with it, he put a curse on us. My cherished friend, Mr. *Bless Me, Ultima*, said: "I hope you have four flat tires in the desert. I hope the car catches fire. I hope it burns to the ground."

Way to go, Ed!

Making friends.

But I too am mad at Ed. I don't know why anybody else is mad at him, and plenty of people are—which, of course, in the post-Abbeyan universe, is all the more reason to love Ed. That's part of the seductiveness of Edward Abbey, isn't it? The world's full of bastards, and Ed will cuss them out for us, tilt at them with his sharpened war lance, be inspected by the FBI, and occasionally blow up a bridge or sodomize a tractor into submission, all the while throwing cleverly hidden poems into his paragraphs and, for no extra charge, making us laugh.

We, in turn, get to feel like we have done battle with wicked forces while hiding behind a dead man. We feel like Ed's pals. Ed speaks for us, we compliment ourselves by thinking. We say Ed is our voice, expressing our deep feelings, after Ed himself often set the agenda we now claim for our own in one of his books that we bought out of a "used" box for $1.45.

Chicano readers, too, could be seduced. Like many people with a cause, we can be essentially pathetic, eager to side with anybody who sounds halfway sympathetic. Our weariness with the struggle, our exhaustion, is what makes us vulnerable. Our exhaustion makes us latch on to a strong voice for justice. And Ed, with his championing of lizards and watersheds, seemed to be championing us, too. Ed made some of us hope. And we fell over like puppies, wagging and peeing at his feet.

This is proof enough for me that Ed was a great writer.

He angers the effete, and he utterly seduces his readers into absorbing his pith as if we were amoebas. And, sometimes, he hurts us.

Edward Abbey once stuck a knife in my heart.

I didn't know him outside of his books, and although I ponder swiping the car now and then, I'm not going to claim any special connection to the man. Or the ghost. Connecting with the books was quite enough. *Desert Solitaire, The Monkey Wrench Gang, Black Sun, The Journey Home* all had a massive, perhaps catastrophic, effect on me. I went mad for Ed, but more important, and a major reason others fell in love with him too, was the aching love he ignited in me for the land. The world. The *tierra*.

Ed Abbey—shaman.

Imagine my shock, and the shock of all of Ed's other Chicano, Mexican, Hispanic readers when we picked up *One Life at a Time, Please* and read the now infamous screed about ourselves, "Immigration and Liberal Taboos." In it, Ed sets down his official policies regarding Mexicans: "They come to stay and they stay to multiply." Or how about this *bon mot* from "egalitarian" Ed: "it might be wise for us as American citizens to consider calling a halt to the mass influx of even more millions of hungry, ignorant, unskilled, and culturally-morally-genetically impoverished people." Morally, Ed? Culturally? *Genetically?* This from a redneck hillbilly from Home, Pennsylvania. About people who had *culture* when his ancestors were dog-styling sheep and digging turnips and cow turds out of the sad mud in their serf villages. Of course, Ed also informed his readers that Latin American societies were societies of "squalor, cruelty, and corruption," while the American vista was one that was "open, spacious, uncrowded, and beautiful—yes, beautiful!"

Ed Abbey—Aryan.

Oh my, Ed, you lying bastard. After writing countless books in which you decry America as just the opposite of free and open—after doing that very thing in the same book—after seducing us with battle cries based on the very spoiling of this land by overcrowded gringo swine, you fall for Pete Wilsonesque scapegoating. The very prospect of teeming brown cockroach-people (to swipe the Brown Buffalo's term) drives you into a hideous U-turn. The thought, apparently, of my people. The thought of me.

Did I remember to mention that writers are hypocrites?

Sitting in Ed's boat, Safeway parking blot, Broadway & Campbell—Tucson. The journey's about to begin. Two blueberry muffins and some styrofoam coffee for breakfast. My candidate for Miss Universe loads groceries into her whining little Coke-can imported car. Ed's Eldorado says AMURCA FURST, BUDDEH! However, Ed's Eldorado does not say "Earth First!" If anything, it probably says "Ed First." Hell yes. Ed's Eldorado remembers Pearl Harbor. The plates say HAYDUKE.

Ed's ghost sits in the back seat. He holds up his letter to the editor, *Arizona Daily Star*, dated Jan. 7, 1982: "I was not talking about 'cultural influences' but about the social and economic effects of unchecked mass immigration from the impoverished nations to our south, particularly Mexico. Certainly Mexico has contributed much to the Southwestern heritage; I like tacos, tequila, and *ranchero* music about as much as anybody else does." Tacos? Tequila? The thing about ghosts is, they don't have to stop at putting their feet in their mouths. They can go ahead and gobble the whole leg, jam it in there all the way down till they've maneuvered their heads up their own asses.

By the way, Ed says, in the introduction to *One Life at a Time, Please*, that "Immigration and Liberal Taboos" is his favorite essay in the book.

Did Ed Abbey hate Mexicans? Or was he really setting out to tweak liberals? I'm trying hard not to do backflips here just to defend my favorite writer. Consider: where many writers have a pitiable need to be loved, Ed seemed to have a puzzling need to be reviled. Puzzling, that is, if one considers Ed Abbey to be merely a *writer*. We all know he was an anarchist, a trickster, an agitator, and an "eco-warrior," whatever that means. In his "A Writer's Credo" (same book), the very first sentence says: "It is my belief that the writer . . . should be and must be a critic of the society in which he lives." Not a word about fame, love, beauty, or literary awards.

Ed Abbey, by his own words, saw himself as a critic, a gadfly. In McGuane's words, "The original fly in the ointment." And nobody was spared. After all, *One Life at a Time, Please* contains his even more infamous assault on "The Cowboy and his Cow."

Perhaps it should not surprise me, then, when in the middle of my outrage over this awful essay, I stumble on a sentiment that I absolutely agree with. Ed suddenly says: "The conservatives love their cheap labor; the liberals love their cheap cause. (Neither group, you will notice, ever invites the immigrants to move into their *homes*. Not into *their* homes!)"

Right on, homey! El Vato Loco Cactus Eddie Y Que Abbey, Barrio Desierto Rifa Con Safos Cabrones, lays down some righteous chingazos for la causa, Ese!

Oh, well.

Some of us are social misfits; we spend vast periods of time locked in rooms banging at typewriters and computers. Those of us who like to write "outdoors" stuff spend even more hours stumbling over rocks and backing into cacti. Alone. Of all the things one could say about Ed, I suspect that nobody would accuse him of being a schmooze-meister. Worse if a writer has a cause. We will burrow through bystanders as if they were dirt clods and we were rabid moles.

Indelicacy follows us through our tunnels. Chicanos, we must admit, have said scabrous and wounding things about *gabachos* in publication after publication. Mexicans say foul things about both *gringos* and Chicanos. The whole lot of us cast a suspicious eye toward Central America and points south.

And, of course, writers carry the baggage of their times, their origins, and their own spiritual and intellectual laziness.

I admire Edward Abbey. I enjoy his books. And I love his bad-taste car—all the way down to its honky-tonk red carpet on the dash. This car is twenty steel feet of Ed's laughter.

I also decry his ignorance and his duplicity.

Guess what: Ed Abbey had feet of clay.

Just like me.

Still, he managed to throw in a closing that resonated with me all down the years. I knew, in a terribly clear way, that he was right. "Stop every *campesino* at our southern border, give him a handgun, a good rifle, and a case of ammunition, and send him home. He will know what to do with our gifts and good wishes. The people know who their enemies are."

Ed's ghost lights a cigar and puts its feet up on the seat back. I ponder this last paragraph as we cross the Luna County Line. A million acres of open desert accrues paper cups and Payday wrappers around us. Flat as a griddle for a few miles, then truculent upheavals of bare naked mountains. To the north, grape-juice rainclouds color the horizon.

Indians and Chicanos, who know a good thing when they see it, catch up to the car and give us the big thumbs-up.

Ed Abbey—lowrider.

The Poetry Center Interview

On February 2, 1977, Edward Abbey read for the University of Arizona Poetry Center's Visiting Writers Series in the Modern Languages Auditorium. Even before Abbey arrived, the seats in the auditorium were filled and latecomers sprawled in both aisles and crowded hallway entrances. Many of them carried copies of *The Monkey Wrench Gang*. When Lois Shelton, director of the Poetry Center, arrived with Abbey at her side, there was some talk of moving the reading elsewhere. Instead, Lois took the podium and asked people sitting in the aisles to move down toward the front of the auditorium. She introduced Abbey and invited the audience to meet the author over punch and cookies after the reading in the Terrace Room of the Student Union.

The applause that greeted Abbey came loud, long, and uproarious. I noticed a department head and an assistant dean standing on their chairs to see Abbey make his way to the stage. Within a few minutes both had left the building along with a small stream of their peers. Their seats were quickly taken, however, by those in the aisles nearest them.

What induced a department head and assistant dean to leave the reading produced a chorus of boos and shouts of encouragement from others in the audience, for Abbey opened the reading with a series of profane love songs he entitled "Love's Bawdy." "I'm not really a professional poet," he told his audience, "but I am living in your poet's cottage this week, so I am your official poet. God knows I've written a lot of poetry, but I've never published any of it anywhere. I think I'll read some of it to you so you'll understand why. . . ."

Mercifully, Abbey kept this part of the reading short. His method was to introduce each "poem" by dedicating it to a woman. Invariably, a woman in the audience by the same name would shriek or scream at the sound of "Ingrid" or "Bonnie" or "Clare" coming over the microphone. "No! Not *that* Clare," Abbey would insist, although he began each poem with an inquiry: "This one's for Ingrid. Is Ingrid here tonight?"

For most of the audience, Abbey's reading entertained and delighted. Others it outraged and incensed and even shocked. Notices in the local press afterwards were typically derogatory, as the opening sentences from even *Mountain Newsreal,* Tucson's most liberal monthly, indicate: "Edward Abbey should have stayed home last week to preserve his image as a cactus jumping Henry David Thoreau," wrote Margaret Hernandez. "Instead he came to Tucson to treat his audience to low-class erotic poetry, boring letters from his fans and his now-trite works condemning urban sprawl and smelter pollution."

As for myself, I was curious enough about Abbey after hearing him read to ask Lois Shelton to schedule an interview for me. Consequently, Lois arranged for Abbey and me to meet the next day over a tape recorder in Robert Houston's undergraduate fiction class. I sent the transcribed interview to Abbey a few weeks later. Although he made a few small changes, what follows is nearly a literal transcription of our conversation.

In conversation Abbey is extraordinarily quiet and shy, a disarming contrast to the public Abbey and the image he has himself helped to create as a boisterous iconoclast. He speaks in low, even tones and listens carefully and attentively to questions. On this occasion he wore a deep blue V-neck sweater over a tan shirt, khaki pants, and low-heeled, round-toed boots.

ABBEY: I'm not responsible for anything I'm about to say.

HEPWORTH: When did you start writing? And how?

ABBEY: I suppose, like most activities, it began in childhood in various forms. I did my own comic books when I was a little kid. I went into journalism when I was in high school. I flunked the course, but I got interested in writing then. I was still interested in writing when I went to college. Sold my first piece about twenty-two years ago, so I feel that I've been at it all my life in one form or another.

HEPWORTH: You mentioned journalism last night. Do you consciously shift gears when you go from one genre to another?

ABBEY: I think I get more serious when I'm trying to write a piece of fiction. Perhaps that's why my fiction has not been so successful. When I'm writing an article or essay, I tend to think it's not very important, so I dash it off freestyle, more or less off the top of my head—or the bottom of my belly. I improvise, just dash along in any old manner that seems suitable to me. When I'm starting a piece of fiction,

I do make a conscious decision about what sort of style I'm going to write it in, as well as what the story is going to be about. I'm not sure that's good, but I think that's been my practice so far.

HEPWORTH: You let the style more or less find itself. Do you think, then, that you have developed a journalistic style without making a conscious decision about it?

ABBEY: My journalistic style is pretty informal, I'd say; when I'm writing a piece of fiction, I tend to get a little more self-conscious, and try to make the style fit the subject matter and vice versa. I think you can see that in the novels that I've written, if you've read them. It seems to me that each one is written in a different style.

HOUSTON: Do you make a distinction between style, tone, and voice?

ABBEY: No, by the word *style*, I mean to include those terms.

HEPWORTH: Who are your favorite contemporary American journalists?

ABBEY: In the field of journalism, I'm a Hunter S. Thompson freak. I do admire his work. I would have to admit I like Tom Wolfe's stuff, too, but I don't like his point of view. And in fiction, I like Tom McGuane. Have you read *Ninety-Two in the Shade? The Bushwacked Piano?* He also wrote the screenplay *Missouri Breaks*, which is kind of well known. A lousy film—I thought—but I like the three novels he's done so far. I'm an admirer of William Eastlake, who used to teach here.

He's also an old friend of mine, but I do think he's a good writer. I think I've learned a lot from him. I see traces of his influence in my stuff. Who else? Pynchon. I like *Gravity's Rainbow*. I didn't understand it, of course, but I was fascinated by it.

In fact, one night I was sitting in my little hut out in Ari-vaipa Canyon when I was a caretaker out there. I was trying to finish *Gravity's Rainbow*. I was on page 780 or so, forty or fifty more pages to go. I was sitting on the couch in my little trailer house out there, and a scorpion crawled out from underneath the couch and stung me on the foot, and I got up and—Oh, I hate to admit it—but I stepped on that poor old scorpion. Got mad. And so I killed the scorpion. Then I went in the kitchen and filled the basin with ice cubes and water and put my stung foot in that basin of icewater and went on and finished the book. I just couldn't stop. Probably by that time I was weighted on compulsion just to get through the damn thing. After you've read 700 pages . . .

HEPWORTH: What about Stegner?

ABBEY: Well, I did read Stegner's biography of Powell, but I don't think I've read any of his fiction. Have you people read a collection called *The Neon Wilderness* by Nelson Algren? They're fine little stories.

HEPWORTH: How about Frank Waters?

ABBEY: Oh, I don't like Waters's style very much. I read *The Man Who Killed the Deer* a long, long time ago, in my student days back in the '50s. It didn't attract me. Something about Waters's style. It's too . . . what? Fancy? Overblown?

HEPWORTH: Romantic?

ABBEY: Yeah. I read the book he wrote about the Colorado River and disliked it for similar reasons. He maintains a constant high pitch and intensity and fine, fancy rhetoric, it seems to me. I prefer writers who can range over a whole scale of tones and voices, who can go from the burlesque to the bawdy to the sublime, poetical. I think Pynchon has that ability. I think that's one reason his books interest me so much.

HEPWORTH: What do you think of Gore Vidal's work?

ABBEY: I like his essays very much. I think he is a brilliant essayist, critic, reviewer. Certainly, I admire his wit, his sharp tongue. I've read a few of his novels and didn't like them very much. He's certainly a competent writer, no question about that. His things are perfectly written, but they seem to lack some sort of basic passion. They're amusing, witty, well done, but he's just not the kind of writer that I very much admire. I like Steinbeck, Céline. I like writers who are sort of half-crazy at best. I think it does help to be crazy, and I think Vidal is much too sane and rational a person to be a great novelist.

HEPWORTH: Do you think the things you've written, particularly your conservation articles published in magazines with enormous readerships like *Playboy* and *Audubon*, have altered the way people think, say, about strip mining?

ABBEY: I doubt it. I don't think written propaganda makes much difference in a war. I got a lot of letters from that article in *Playboy* you're referring to, both pro and con. I was very flattered to get hate letters from Senator Hanson of Wyoming and from Senator Moss of Utah, from the president of the American Coal Association and an official of the EPA . . . all those fellows wrote in condemning the article, which was quite delightful to me, of course.

HEPWORTH: How about *Monkey Wrench Gang?* Have you had much response from that?

ABBEY: No, no official reaction at all.

HEPWORTH: Are the characters in that book inspired by real people?

ABBEY: Yes, to some extent. You might say they are inspired by people I know. They're not portraits of anybody I know. I borrowed a lot of things for each of those people: attitudes, style of language, occupations, even physical appearance. But I would still insist that they are not portraits. I just borrowed what was useful to create the fictional characters.

HEPWORTH: Is there a movie in the process for that book?

ABBEY: There's an option on the book. Whether they'll actually raise the money to make a film out of it, I don't know. Hollywood options far more books than they ever get around to filming.

HOUSTON: How do you feel they did by you with *Lonely Are the Brave?*

ABBEY: I like that film. I think that they did pretty well. Dalton Trumbo wrote the screenplay. He followed the book.

He didn't change the story very much. They deleted a lot of the long-winded, philosophizing dialogue, jail cell scenes. I think they made a good movie.

HEPWORTH: Did you consider taking a part in it?

ABBEY: I did have a part in it. I was one of the sheriff's deputies. I still get a check every year from the Screen Actor's Guild for about $4.55. As long as they keep running it on TV I guess I'll receive one.

HEPWORTH: Did they ask you to script the movie?

ABBEY: No, I was hurt by that. They bought that book several years after it was published. They only paid me $7,500 for it. I think they felt a little guilty about that. When they began filming it, they hired me as a consultant. I persuaded them to use the Albuquerque, New Mexico, setting for the actual filming, same as in the story, so they hired me to show them around the town, show them where the roads and trails were in the mountains, out on West Mesa. It was the best job I ever had in my life. They paid me $100 a day and all expenses. Of course, the job only lasted three days. And they also gave me this bit part and a sheriff's deputy's costume, a leather jacket and a gun full of blanks. No speaking part.

HOUSTON: Do you market your own stuff?

ABBEY: No, I've got an agent in New York. . . . He's the only agent I've ever had. I've had a few publishers complain to me about what a ruthless man he is, so I guess he's good.

HOUSTON: When you do non-fiction, do you go looking for ideas? Do you say, "Hey, I need six or seven hundred bucks. It's time to do an article!" Or do you just write when you feel like writing?

ABBEY: Well, ever since I published *Desert Solitaire*, I've been writing magazine articles on commission. The editors approach me. That's how I sort of got stuck in this rut—because of that one book. I never wanted to be an environmental crusader, an environmental journalist. I wanted to be a fiction writer, a novelist. Then I dashed off that *Desert Solitaire* thing because it was easy to do. All I did was copy out of some journals that I'd kept. It was the first book that I published that had any popularity at all, and at once I was put into the "Western Environmentalist Writer" bag, category, pigeonhole. I haven't tried very hard to get out of it. I've been making a pretty easy living at it since then.

HOUSTON: You don't really mind taking the commissions as they come up? You don't ever say, "No. That doesn't interest me"?

ABBEY: I've turned down a few. Not very many. Time-Life wanted me to write a book about the Okeechobee Swamp. I decided to hell with that.

HEPWORTH: Is publishing fiction a problem for you? As you said yourself a moment ago, your work has been pigeonholed. We tend to think of you as an environmentalist writer. Don't publishers tend to demand more of the same, more of what will sell?

ABBEY: I haven't had that problem yet. I've been able to publish most of the fiction I've written. Most of the fiction, too, has had a western or southwestern setting. It's been, at least to some extent, concerned with environmental issues, I guess you could say. I haven't been able to avoid that. The novel I'm trying to finish is a futuristic western set in Phoenix about the year 1999, after The Great Collapse. Horses are grazing on Van Buren, Gila monsters scampering up and down Central Avenue.

HEPWORTH: Is that a wistful vision or a frightening vision?

ABBEY: The way my story is going, there's a massive struggle going on over the control of Phoenix, over whether or not Phoenix should be rebuilt. Some are trying to help Phoenix rise from its ashes. The other faction is trying to finish burning it down. It's about a regional civil war.

HOUSTON: Are you taking sides?

ABBEY: Implicitly. I suppose you could call it a novel of political ideas, essentially. Anarchy versus Order.

HOUSTON: But you're not trying to tell us which side you're on?

ABBEY: Well, I'm trying to be fair, trying not to stack the deck—too much.

HEPWORTH: Are you satisfied with your writing?

ABBEY: I keep hoping I can do better. I have the feeling that I've never put my best effort into a book. Maybe that's illusion. It seems to me everything I've written has been too easy, did not require much effort.

HEPWORTH: Last night during your reading you said something to the effect that every novelist fancies himself a poet. Do you read poetry? Do you write poetry seriously?

ABBEY: Oh, yes! I've written a lot of very serious, very intense poetry, and I was tempted to try that out on you last night. Chickened out. I don't think any of it was good enough to try to publish, but I would like to write poetry. I think maybe I could.

HEPWORTH: Do you think the reading public and publishers themselves are more receptive than they used to be to fiction written about the West?

ABBEY: I don't know. I think it is still a handicap to write about the West. It's hard to get critics and reviewers to take any book with a western setting seriously. They're always tempted to dismiss it as some kind of *western* literature, much as women's books are dismissed: "Oh, here's another Women's Book. . . . " Once you give a book a western setting and you fail to populate it with stereotypes, publishers might not be so interested. If you're going to write a serious book about big city life, well, they would say, then you had better get back to New York. We may be able to overcome that, eventually.

HEPWORTH: How?

ABBEY: Well, I think Eastlake has had some success at it. I think his novels are taken quite seriously by the eastern critics. Of course, he was also smart enough to write a couple of war novels to show that he could do that, too.

HOUSTON: Eastlake always comes down on the "right" side, too. His characters aren't bad, but his Indians are what publishers want to hear about Indians. . . .

ABBEY: Yeah, his Indians are fantasy creatures. . . .

HEPWORTH: Probably no other two groups have been any more affected by prevaricated models of themselves than the American Indian and the Anglo born or raised in the West.

ABBEY: Yeah. Some Vietnam war veterans have told me that the most popular TV show in Vietnam was *Combat*. They said many of the soldiers used to sit around the set and watch the series to see how it was done, see how they were supposed to talk. Go to any small town drugstore. You'll see all the paperbacks are westerns.

HEPWORTH: Yes. Even the people who should know better still refuse to see the West as anything other than the Last Frontier.

ABBEY: I guess the westering myth is the nearest thing to a national myth we can ever create in the country. It's very possible. It may never be possible to overcome it, or get away from it. Maybe it's not even desirable. Maybe literary historians five hundred years from now will decide that Zane Grey and Louis L'Amour were the most important American writers.

HEPWORTH: Did I hear you say you once taught writing?

ABBEY: I presided over a writing sweatshop up in Salt Lake City one time. I only tried it that once. Maybe I could do it better with a little experience. I didn't quite feel I was giving the kids their money's worth. I could read their stuff and say, "This is all right, or this is terrible, or . . . " I don't have any analytical or critical talent for pointing to exactly what's wrong with somebody's work, for telling them how to improve it. I also found it hard to get interested. I got discouraged. One poor guy, I'm sure, I discouraged from writing forever. He wrote a Mormon love story. I read it aloud to the class. (It was my policy to read everybody's work myself, and in that way it could get a fair and impartial reading.) I read this guy's Mormon love story, and I couldn't help laughing at all the wrong places. For half the story the hero agonized over whether or not to kiss the girl.

HEPWORTH: Some writers wake up and they find out that the public knows who they are, that they have a kind of image or myth they're supposed to live up to. All of a sudden, some writers who find this out start playing games. Does your recognition ever tempt you or ever bother you?

ABBEY: Oh, I'm dimly aware of some sort of mythical Edward Abbey, but I don't take him seriously, don't attempt to live up to it. I'm surprised that anyone would ever want to meet me because I don't live up to the characters in my books, don't try to. It sometimes seems to me that the Edward Abbey who writes these articles and books and so on is just another fictional creation, not much resemblance to the real one, to the one I think I know. The real Edward Abbey—whoever the hell that is—is a real shy, timid fellow, but the character I create in my journalism is perhaps a person I would like to be: bold, brash, daring. I created this character, and I gave him my name. I guess some people mistake the creation for the author, but that's their problem.

597ax

This is a dreadful room. Of course, every classroom I've seen here is dreadful—the same greyish-white walls, the same tan cork bulletin boards covered with advertisements for research-paper services and *Time* and evenings of introduction to Transcendental Meditation. In the worst of them the desks are bolted to the floor and the students sit trapped in rows staring at the backs of one another's heads. In the best, the seminar rooms, students sitting around grey formica tables in turquoise vinyl chairs may at least look one another in the face. This room is halfway between—the desks grip one in the middle tight as jaws, but at least they're movable. In theory, we could push them into a circle and face each other; in practice, we leave them in ragged rows and stare ahead at the teacher.

He stands at the front of the room gravely. In my journal I jot, "Rugged. Handsome. Grey-bearded." Just my image of a park ranger. He writes long lists on the chalkboard, which we copy into notebooks.

He recommends magazines: *The New Yorker, The New York Review of Books, Atlantic, Harper's, Esquire, Nation, New Republic, National Review, Mother Jones, Rocky Mountain Magazine, Outside.*

He recommends essayists: Montaigne, Orwell, White, Thoreau.

He asks us to buy, read, and review three of the following: Edward Hoagland, *Reader*; Joan Didion, *Slouching Toward Bethlehem*, *The White Album*; Nora Ephron, *Scribble, Scribble*; Joseph Wood Krutch, *Best Nature Writing*, *Krutch Omnibus*; John McPhee, *Reader*; Alan Harrington, *The Immortalist*, *Psychopaths*; Wendell Berry, *The Long-Legged House*, *The Unsettling of America*; Barry Lopez, *Of Wolves and Men*, *Desert Notes, River Notes*; Michael Herr, *Dispatches*; Hunter Thompson, *Fear and Loathing in Las Vegas*, *The Great Shark Hunt*; Tom Wolfe, *The Right Stuff*, *Mauve Gloves . . .*; James Baldwin, *Notes of a Native Son*; Edward Abbey, *Abbey's Road*, *The Journey Home*; Lewis Thomas, *The Lives of a Cell*, *The Medusa and the Snail*; Annie Dillard, *Pilgrim at Tinker Creek*; Norman Mailer, *Presidential Papers*, *Cannibals and Christians*; William Zinsser, *On Writing Well*.

When he has finished the lists, he asks by way of dismissal, "Are there any questions?"

Everyone looks blank. Notebook paper shuffles. Then someone says, "Yes. What should we call you?"

"Mr. Abbey," he says. "You should call me Mr. Abbey."

In return he calls us Ms. Mairs, Mr. Kessler, Mr. Moneyhun, Mr. Hepworth, Ms. Miller, Mr. Barwell. . . . Perhaps he has been told, as I was my first year of teaching, that one must run a class on a last-name basis in order to maintain respect. Or perhaps he is imitating, as most teachers do, the pedagogical style of his own professors.

I don't like to be called Ms. Mairs. A few people call me Mrs. Mairs—those students who still believe that some pigs are more equal than others, and the women on the telephone who try to sell me carpet-cleaning for my carpetless house. But I don't like titles, which reinforce distinctions and distances among people, thereby creating space for patterns of domination; and I refer to myself only as Nancy. I don't know if any of my classmates share my political objections, but they must be a little baffled at the formality—manners are pretty casual at this university, as I guess they're bound to be anywhere that the climate permits students to come to class more than half-naked most of the year. Once I've seen a student's navel, I find it hard to call him "Mr. Holmes."

The matter of names presents a tonal problem, but the class has structural difficulties as well. For one thing, we have no texts. In other workshops, we hand out copies of our work the week before discussing them, but here we read them aloud. I write in my journal, "Abbey's workshop. I like being entertained by people reading to me aloud, but I can't possibly retain enough of what I hear to offer any criticism." The penalty for literacy—for turning composition into a written rather than an oral art—is that we no longer learn to listen as acutely as we read. In consequence, discussion here tends to be vague, desultory.

The problem is exacerbated by the motley make-up of the group. Most of the members are in the M.F.A. program, but some write poetry and some fiction. A couple of us, having taken the M.F.A., are working toward the Ph.D. A couple more are undergraduates, wide-eyed young women who drop out before the end of the semester—daunted, perhaps, by the amount of work required. Three to six typewritten pages due every Monday, including the three book reviews, a magazine review, and an interview. Edward Abbey doesn't fool around.

Such a mixture could be enlivening, but it isn't. At this university—maybe at every such institution—division is the underlying principle. Artists from scientists, "creative writers" from "critics," poets from fiction-writers from essayists.

If you try to straddle, you're likely to end up drawn and quartered. This class operates on just such a principle. One of the members will later say to me in a letter, "The answer [to his difficulty in finding a teaching job] lies in separating writing instruction from English Departments altogether. I'd like to quarantine the lit. people in separate Literature Depts. Perhaps these can be integrated into departments of Archeology or even Museum Science, if there is such a thing." Everyone here is a little suspicious of what everyone else is doing.

I know all these things because I've been a graduate student here enough years that my longevity is an embarrassment. Edward Abbey has just come.

Whether because of the strain of formality or the lack of texts or the motley membership, the class isn't working. One day we move to The Big A, a beer-and-hamburger joint near campus, where we sit around a long wooden table facing each other; but one of us tells the English Department, and it turns out that meeting off-campus violates university regulations. So we squeeze back into our desks, drooping and drowsing in our stuffy fluorescent room.

Complaints about the class have begun almost immediately, the kind of generalized bitching that makes me furious. Especially when it's done by graduate students, who bear a heavy responsibility, it seems to me, when a class goes badly. I am more patient with teacher-dependence in my freshmen. But we're not bewildered freshmen. Several of us, in fact, are experienced and capable teachers. It's up to us, I tell some of the gripers, to make the class work.

I don't exactly put my money where my mouth is. I've been messing up my life, and I've withdrawn now to the remotest corner of myself, where I spend a lot of time gazing out of the window at a couple of trees against the dark-rose bricks of the College of Education and jotting down acerbic notes in my journal. "Earth-maiden . . . has brought her dog, who whistles in his sleep or wanders around, nails clicking on the linoleum." "Alan Harrington, author of *The Immortalist*, is here. We are talking about the possibility of living forever. Not something of lively interest to a suicide." "Clyde has read a piece on Indians. Some discussion of 'Indians,' limited to a few people. Jim says, 'It's too late to leave the Apaches alone.' Let's. Let's leave the Apaches alone." Later I will feel sorry for my tightness, my distance, my lack of generosity.

Slowly the class begins to improve. We seem not so wary of each other, and we are working out ways of discussing pieces we only hear. Ed relaxes, his shyness now natural and close-fitting, not a piece of armor. One day he reads us his own work, an essay on Arivaipa Canyon which will appear later in *Down the River*, and we are reassured of his involvement in the struggle. It's late, but we've begun the process of supporting one another in our work. I begin to think that textlessness has advantages. The focus in most workshops is too often narrow, nitpicking, negative, a piece scrutinized for its shortcomings rather than its successes. Here our vision is necessarily diffuse, our responses impressionistic and global. We act as appreciators of one another's ventures, a true audience.

Uncertain at the outset in the classroom, Ed is from the first a sure-handed editor, thorough, tough, and good-humored. This last quality I tax to the extreme. New to prose-writing, except for academic purposes, and engaged in the study of women's autobiography, I use this class to buy time for experimentation. I start generating a dreary, static reminiscence of a house in my childhood, which I dole out in dribs and drabs, whatever I've written in a week. After the first drib, Ed writes, "Keep going with it." After the second, he's getting itchy: "Dear Ms. Mairs, this stuff is getting too vague, a bit boring. . . . What's your point? . . . You need some laughs in this here opus. And—contrary to Nabokov—some *ideas.* Of course you can't please everybody, but in *this* course you have only to please me." At the end of twenty pages, he's done in: "I can understand that your reminiscences seem precious to you, as mine do to me, but somehow you've got to find a way, a device, a meaning, to make these memoirs readable to an ordinary bored, busy, hard-nosed, cynical, weary, cigar-smoking, whisky-drinking, fornicating old fart like—not me!—but your typical magazine or book editor. In its present form it will not sell. Maybe you don't care about that, and that's okay, but still, your primary obligation as a writer is to give pleasure, to entertain, or at least to instruct. Now if you were (already) a famous person this might not matter; but you're not; so it does." I'm exhausted too.

But I don't reform. I do a couple of short pieces—and they work—and then suddenly, grief-stricken at the death of a kitten, I'm spewing a lifetime of memories of cats. Ed likes cats, and he bears up well. But finally he has to plead for mercy: "OK, very charming, but this cat saga is getting too long & complicated. Why not dash off the assigned book reviews, and the interview, as requested, and we'll call it quits for 597ax 1981." If I were he, I don't think I could be so polite in the face of certain death by smothering in parti-colored fur.

It's almost the end of the semester, and Ed is looking decidedly haggard. He's been teaching three workshops a week—the other two for undergraduates—and no doubt ed-

iting all the submissions with the same painstaking attention
he's given to mine. Nine hours a week in the classroom, probably three times that wielding a red pencil. When, I wonder,
does he do any work of his own?

Probably never, if my experience is any gauge. Writing
and teaching are two of the most incompatible activities I
know, because they eat up the same sort of creative energy,
require the same imaginative structuring of experience for
an audience. What you give to your students—and if you're
any good, you give a hell of a lot—you don't have left for the
blank page. And teaching is seductive, because the audience
is live. They respond. They draw more and more out of you,
tap more and more of your reserves, the time and effort you
meant to spend elsewhere, elsewhen. If you let them. I let
them, and I know a lot of other writers who do too.

Perhaps any work other than writing is bad for the writer:
Melville suffered, no doubt, on account of the bills of lading;
and T. S. Eliot had to be bought out of the bank by his
friends. But, having done other things, I think teaching especially dangerous. And nowadays, with writing programs
and workshops and conferences flourishing, an increasing
number of writers are getting sucked into it. Some resolve
the dilemma by teaching badly: reading students' manuscripts sloppily or not at all, dashing off hasty and superficial
comments, holding classes erratically. Most, too conscien-
tious for such an easy resolution, live like jugglers, trying to
keep the poem, the novel, the essay from smashing into the
ground.

Desert Solitaire wasn't jotted down on Monday afternoons
after two and a half hours of 597ax. Nor was *The Monkey
Wrench Gang*. If some of *Down the River* gets written during
this semester, it does so despite, not because of, Clyde's Indi-

ans and my cats. The better teacher Ed becomes, the more tempted I am to burst into his office, shouting and shooing: "Off with you! Now! Go breach a dam. Lock the door behind you. And lose the key."

End of the semester. We're all looking a little haggard now, as everyone does at the end of fifteen weeks of teaching/writing. The last day of class, English Department policy be damned, we gather at Ed and Clarke's house on the desert's edge and drink beer. Away from the fluorescent lights, the pink and green plastic desks, with the promise of a long break only a week away, we seem buoyant in spite of the sudden heat that leaves you gasping in surprise, spring after spring, in this immoderate climate.

A handful of us are left at dinner time, so we grill some hot dogs over a fire on the patio and wrap them in tortillas and wash them down with more beer. The sun has pitched over the edge of the Tucsons, leaving their saw-toothed profile flat and purplish against the greening sky. Venus pricks through, not far from a sliver of moon. I suppose we talk, but later when I picture the scene it will be a silent still, a few blurred blue silhouettes against the coming stars.

Finally we scatter. In the calm air outside the city sounds seem thin and sharp, car doors slamming, voices calling. "Goodnight." "Goodnight." "Great party." "See you soon." "Goodnight." "Thanks, Ed."

The Angry Lover

The warnings are there, clear back to 1878 when John Wesley Powell's *Report on the Arid Lands of the United States* made its point that western rangelands differ from eastern farmlands in that without irrigation they are worthless for agriculture. There followed an illustrious line of ecological spokesmen, including Theodore Roosevelt, John C. Van Dyke, Robinson Jeffers, Paul Sears, Bernard DeVoto, J. Frank Dobie, Justice William O. Douglas, Joseph Wood Krutch, David Brower, and most recently, Edward Abbey—theirs a chorus of concern rising to anger.

All shades of feeling are in their works, beginning with the bare statistics of Major Powell and the blunt advice of President Roosevelt. Van Dyke was the first to perceive the automobile as a litterer. Jeffers foretold doom for the despoilers. While DeVoto slashed and Dobie scorned, Sears warned in *Deserts on the March* and Krutch lectured that man rends the natural fabric at his own peril. Brower led the Sierra Club's attack on dam builders and strip miners.

Then came Edward Abbey, avowed philosophical anarchist, whose *Desert Solitaire* exploded in 1968 as the angriest of all demands for an end to "development." As a former park employee he opposed the Park Service's program of opening up the domains with more roads. He wrote from experience as a seasonal ranger in the Arches National Monument in Utah.

National parks and monuments for whom, the few or the many? For those, Abbey declared, who will make the effort to walk, bicycle, or ride horseback; otherwise there will finally be no parks for either the few or the many, for nature cannot withstand motorized man, witness Yosemite's midsummer madness and the bumper-to-bumper parade through Yellowstone.

To call Edward Abbey the Thoreau of the West is no misnomer. Like the Yankee dissenter he wants to be no more than his own self. Even when Abbey writes of backpacking or riverboating with others, the reader is aware of his isolated identity.

When *Desert Solitaire* appeared I was immured on a New England campus. It made me more restless than angry, and reconfirmed me as a Westerner. The book was acrid with the smell of the big sage—*artemesia tridentata*—and hot with the author's favorite dish of scrambled eggs and green chili. *Come home*, the book said to me, *you don't belong east of the Cimarrón*.

I recalled Abbey's earlier novels, *The Brave Cowboy* (1956) and *Fire on the Mountain* (1962). A rereading disclosed the buildup of pressure that had erupted in *Desert Solitaire*. Abbey had long been on collision course with bureaucratic society. It was not astonishing to find that his 1959 M.A. thesis at the University of New Mexico was entitled "Anarchism and the Morality of Violence."

I was only briefly tempted to write about Edward Abbey. To write on living writers is risky, for there is no way of knowing what they will do next. Their masterpiece may come at the very end as Comfort's did in *Apache*, or at the beginning, witness La Farge's *Laughing Boy*. I had no intention of passing judgment on that youngster, Ed Abbey, born as recently as 1927 and whose star seemed to be still rising.

I hadn't reckoned on an encounter with his newest book. When I read *Cactus Country*, written for the Time-Life Wilderness series about the Sonoran Desert, I learned that Abbey had left New Mexico and Utah for Arizona and was now my neighbor in Tucson. It seemed likely that our trails would cross.

Cactus Country supplements Krutch's books of the same region, although Abbey is more emotional and poetical and less academic than his elder. The novelist is never far off stage. *Cactus Country* is more restrained than *Desert Solitaire*. The reason there is less anger in it, Abbey was to tell me later, is because there is less to be angry about in southwestern Arizona.

Again his experiences as a seasonal ranger, this time in Organ Pipe National Monument, gave the book its substance. There are also chapters on the Kofas, the Pinacate lava fields, and the Gran Desierto. The high point (in the double sense) is an ascent of Baboquívari.

I learned that Ed Abbey had moved again and was now the ranger on a wildlife preserve in the Galiuros northeast of Tucson. I settled in to seek him first in the University Library's holdings of books and periodicals. I was still wary of writing about someone as young and fertile as Abbey. Most writers want only to be praised, and I was also chary of that disillusioning gulf which often lies between the man and his work. Not much has been written about Abbey, probably because he has never stayed put long enough to draw a bead on him.

In a paperback of *Desert Solitaire* I came on this laconic bit of autobiography: "Born in 1927, raised on a farm in Penn-

sylvania, pressed into the infantry in the spring of '45, re-
leased two years later still a private; went to school at Indiana
State Teachers College (one year), University of New Mexico (six years), Edinburgh (one year), and Yale (two weeks).
The army made an anarchist out of me and what with one
thing and another I've been living off the government ever
since."

That move from east to west intrigued me. I found the
answer in an article in *American West*. It told of how in the
summer of 1944, aged seventeen, Abbey had hitchhiked west
to Seattle, down the coast to San Francisco, and via the San
Joaquin Valley (with a look at Saroyan's home in Fresno)
to Needles, and thence via boxcar, thumb, and bus back to
the farm in the Alleghenies near the hamlet appropriately
called Home.

I learned also that Abbey first saw the Southwest (with a
one-night stopover in the Flagstaff city jail) from the open
door of a Santa Fe boxcar. There is still more about that
youthful journey in *Slickrock*, written by Abbey for the Sierra
Club about the canyonlands of southeastern Utah, illustrated from photographs by Philip Hyde.

"I had seen the southern fringe of the canyon country,"
Abbey wrote, "and did not forget it. For the next three years
in the army I kept bright in my remembrance, as the very
picture of things which are free, decent, and sane, what I had
seen and felt—yes, and even smelled—on that one blazing
afternoon on a freight train rolling across northern Arizona.
In 1947 I returned to the Southwest and began to make my
first timid, tentative explorations toward the center of that
beautiful blank space on the maps. From my base at the University of New Mexico, where I would be trying, more or
less, for the next ten years, off and on, to win a degree, I drove
my old Chevie through mud and snow, brush and sand, to

such places as Cabezon on the Puerco and from there south to Highway 66. They said there was no road. They were right."

It was a jackrabbit quest as I zigzagged after Abbey from publisher to publisher, in and out of periodicals, tracking down his articles on such odd subjects as Hoboken, New Jersey, and the Great Barrier Reef of Australia. He seemed uncertain whether he was an academic or an outdoor man. At one point he turned up at Stanford in a creative writing course with Wallace Stegner, then as a teacher of freshman English at the University of Western Carolina and resident writer at the University of Utah.

His career recalled Steinbeck's up to 1939 and his great watershed book of the Okies, after which everything ran downhill to the Nobel Prize, burnout, and death.

Must the price of success be crackup, as it has for so many of our writers? What would a runaway bestseller cost Abbey? Are his western roots as deep as Frank Waters's have proved to be?

In pondering these questions I recalled Steinbeck's once saying to me, after his first three books had failed to sell, "I want a sale of 10,000 copies and no more. That will make enough for my publisher to encourage him to publish another book and will give me enough to live on while I write it, and I'll be able to go on living obscurely." He never had his wish. Thereafter his books were successful beyond count and he became a famous public figure.

I found myself wanting to talk with Abbey as I once had with the young Steinbeck. I wanted to know where Abbey thought he was, on the trajectory of his career. And yet I was reluctant to seek a meeting. A writer's work is writing, not talking about it.

Upon reading Abbey's elusive first novel, *Jonathan Troy*, I saw in it no presage of the books to come, unless it were the sheer vitality of its prose. A book of growing up in a community of farms and coke mills northeast of Pittsburgh, Pennsylvania, *Jonathan Troy* is filled with echoes of Wolfe, Faulkner, and Joyce. It was written when Edward Abbey was in his mid-twenties as a Fulbright Fellow at the University of Edinburgh, and its virtue is its vigor.

Then came an unexpected novel called *The Brave Cowboy*, a morality laid in and around Albuquerque and as much a departure from the orthodox western as *The Oxbow Incident* by Walter Van Tilburg Clark. Abbey sold it to the movies for $7500, and it was made into *Lonely Are the Brave*, starring Kirk Douglas. This was followed by another radical change of pace. *Fire on the Mountain* is a novel told from a twelve-year-old boy's viewpoint of his grandfather's loss of his ranch to the White Sands Missile Range.

Abbey kept on writing unexpected books. His fourth novel, *Black Sun*, is a romance of an aging firewatcher on the North Rim of the Grand Canyon and his love for a nineteen-year-old girl from back east. I read it there in autumn, and the beauty was heightened by the book. It is a tale of the Kaibab forest, the river crossing at Marble Canyon, and the chasm in burning summertime. There is no anger in it; only joy and love, fulfillment and loss, caught in a magic web of language.

This same bemused mood marks an essay on Hoboken which appeared incongruously in *Natural History*. During the 1960s Abbey lived there for two years, commuting as a technical writer for General Electric in Manhattan and as a welfare worker in Brooklyn. Eggs and green chili were replaced by the "bitter bread of exile." What held him was his marriage to an artist who regarded New York as the center of the art world. The essay was written after exile (and marriage) had ended and he was back in the Southwest, living at Lukeville on the edge of the Organ Pipe National Monument.

Abbey's belief that our National Parks should not be opened wide with more roads invigorates *Appalachian Wilderness, the Great Smoky Mountains,* illustrated with Eliot Porter's photographs. Abbey's text includes this statement of his wilderness philosophy: "Speed shrinks distance. Roads shrivel parks. Keep out the cars and you will make what is now a two-hour routine drive from Gatlinburg to Cherokee into something more like a two- or three-day expedition on foot, bicycle, or horseback. Set a man on foot at the entrance to the park, with no means to proceed except by his own energy or inclination, and he faces a vista as wild and immense as that which confronted Hernando de Soto, William Bartram, or Daniel Boone."

An elitist philosophy, it has been called by the proponents of development. Abbey would not argue the point. Like Jeffers he prefers nature to most people.

With my homework done, I set out on a winter morning under the blue Arizona sky to meet Abbey. My companion was Dr. Laurence M. Gould, the university's distinguished geoscientist who is also a member of the advisory board of the George Whittell Wildlife Preserve, owned by the Nature Conservancy, and administered by Defenders of Wildlife. There Edward Abbey was one of two resident rangers.

On the sixty-five-mile drive our talk was of books, for although I do know a mountain from a molehill, to me a rock is a rock is a rock; and my colleague's knowledge of books is deeper than their bindings. As Byrd's first officer on the Antarctic expedition of 1927, Gould lived a book-man's dream of endless night for reading, during which he all but memorized *Green Mansions* and *Leaves of Grass*.

And so I was content to drive and listen, while we rounded the Santa Catalinas, climbed to oak and pine at Oracle, then dropped into the mesquite valley of the San Pedro and trailed along the river-course under a cloud from the smelter at San Manuel.

Our destination was Aravaipa Creek which comes curving out of the Galiuros to empty into the San Pedro a few miles from its junction with the Gila. We ascended the creek on a graded road high above golden cottonwoods to find Abbey's place at the end of the road—a mobile home on a ridge, looking down on the ranch buildings of the Wood brothers, Cliff and Fred. After fifty years of running cattle on lands homesteaded and added to by their father, they sold their 77,000 acres for preservation as a wildlife refuge rather than development by absentee capitalists. This offered Abbey the kind of job every young writer dreams of.

While Gould and Abbey talked geology, beginning with the Arches region where the former had done his fieldwork half a century ago and had written to Senator Reed Smoot of Utah and to Director Horace Albright of the National Park Service, urging government protection of the unique area, I sought to bring Abbey and his work into focus.

The man is tall, powerful and relaxed, bearded and blue-eyed, with a radiant smile. He looks more the lover of *Black Sun* than the anarchist of *Desert Solitaire*. His walls are pinned with topographical maps, illustrations from *Slickrock*, and drawings by Suzi, his little daughter by a second marriage which left him a widower.

My colleague had brought along colored geological maps of the Galiuros, and he and Abbey were soon in deep discussion of the local strata. Were they limestone, sandstone or tuff, that rock welded by volcanic ash? They look alike. Tuff, the maps told them. It is an ancient range, weathered by wind and rain.

I pondered my own questions, awaiting the moment when landscape would yield to literature and find me on familiar ground. After a lunch of bread and cheese and ham, date cake and tea, we set out in a four-wheel drive up from the creek-bed to the base of Table Mountain, at 6,200 feet a high point of the range. The way was steep, narrow and rough, fit only for a big-tired, low-geared vehicle—or a goat. The lands that form the Refuge had been grazed in rotation and are covered with grasses, shrubs and trees, and are alive with quail and dove. The difference between controlled and uncontrolled grazing was evident on each side of a fence line where we stopped to open a locked gate.

On and up we crawled. While my companions looked and talked, I looked and listened. The afternoon deepened, the shadows grew. We rested on a hogback at a windmill where, with the aid of a witcher, water had been struck at 620 feet. The clear air was growing cold. Far to the southeast we saw a blue smudge—the beginnings of the Pinalenos, rising to Mount Graham. Under a veil below in the west lay the San Pedro. In the northwest was the gap in the Pinals through which the Gila breaks on its final run to the Colorado. It is a subtle landscape less likely to attract people than the flamboyant canyonlands of Utah. Abbey's face was blissful.

"Are you staying?" I asked him.

"If you mean here," he answered, "no, not forever. If you mean the Southwest, yes, forever."

"What if Steinbeck had stayed?"

"He wouldn't have been Steinbeck if he had."

"What would you do if you hit it rich the way he did?"

Abbey smiled. "Travel a bit—with a roundtrip ticket— and provide for my children. I've also got two sons by my first marriage."

"'Hostages to fortune,' Bacon said."

Abbey said nothing and I continued. "What else would you do?"

"Buy a piece of land like this, stock it with wildlife and keep people out. And I'd build a house of the native stone— I'll show you where—and then watch the sun rise and set."

"You wouldn't stop writing."

"Not until all the books are out of me."

"How many more?"

"Maybe half a dozen."

"Don't write what the publishers call 'a major novel.'"

Gould had returned at that point from a reconnoitering and demanded, "Do you mean he can't write a *War and Peace?*"

Abbey laughed. "I made the mistake of beginning to read it on my honeymoon. After three nights my wife asked, 'How about me?'"

"What are you writing now?"

"I'm halfway through a novel about a wooden shoe fac- tory. I'm writing about people, not rocks and bushes. They wanted me to go on writing *Desert Solitaire* over and over. I've got a novel about New York no publisher wants."

"You need a western publisher," I said. "When is your best time to write?"

"Early morning—if I don't go out on the porch. Then I get to looking and don't want to work."

"Does it come easy?"

"If I write every day it does. If I don't, it's hard to start again. Here the trouble is that it should be an ideal place for a writer. That's what overwhelms you, the country itself. I should have stayed in Hoboken; I'd be books ahead."

"Do you mean that the best environment for a writer," Gould asked, "is where he is the unhappiest?"

"Well, I was certainly productive in Hoboken!"

"Why didn't you stay in academic work?" I asked.

"I wasn't smart enough. When I went to Yale for a Ph.D. I lasted only two weeks."

"What happened?"

"I took symbolic logic!"

"Why did you want a Ph.D.?"

"Status, I suppose, false ambition."

We started back down the mountain.

Abbey braked to a halt and pointed. There across a *barranca* came a herd of javelina, twenty strong, trotting in single file, the little wild pigs threading a trail, then vanishing into a manzanita thicket. Abbey's face was serene.

We continued our silent descent. It was that clairvoyant time toward evening when life, landscape and literature conjoin. In that moment of clarity I knew the answers to all I had ever pondered and, moreover, felt capable of expressing it with convincing lucidity.

"I am about to inform you, gentlemen," I began, "of what is wrong with our literature."

Again Abbey braked to a halt. "That's Whitewash Canyon. Here's where I'd build my house if I owned this land. Look at that stone!"

Our view was across to rose and buff cliffs with a lens-like intrusion. Far below, the colored trees marked the bed of the Aravaipa.

I tried again. "The trouble is . . ." I stopped when I saw neither was listening.

The geologist began to speak softly, almost to himself. "You'll never find a better example of an intrusion. See how it diminishes into the lens edge. I should have brought my Leica."

"Deer too," Abbey mused. "Lots of them, but unless they move, you need a hawk's eye to spot them. Last week I saw my first Townsend's Solitaire. I wouldn't have known what it was. The Audubon man told me. An ordinary bird, I thought. Pretty though." Abbey turned to me. "You were saying?"

"Oh, to hell with it!" I muttered.

He grinned and eased off the brake. It was darkening when we reached the creekbed and forded the stream, guided by the bare white trunks of the sycamores.

Abbey, Edward: Hellraiser

There's an evening, about first frost, when the elk begin to whistle and bugle in the meadows behind my summer cabin. Aspens fade to a thin lime-green, soon to flash yellow in the autumn winds that fall off the Tetons. The Park Service calls this COB. Culmination of Business. Time to lay off the seasonals.

We seasonals hear the elk and begin to pack for the great migration. For some, COB means winter in Florida, Arizona, Mexico, further. For others it means a winter job indoors, or unemployment. Ski season or school season.

Culmination of Business on my thirteenth season as a park ranger. Elk bugling in the meadows behind the cabin and I'm thinking of Ed. Park Service splits all things of value with commas, the better to fit the proper form. Park Service calls him Abbey comma Edward. Seasonals call him Raiser comma Hell.

Enter on Duty, first season in the Park Service. Laborer comma seasonal. Wage grade one. Cleaner of toilets. Lured from the Midwest, where I was supposed to spend the summer as a counselor at a local mental health camp. Hadn't even heard of Ed, who would later become my teacher at the University of Arizona, a coffeeshop companion for chats about the desert, the mountains, the Park Service. Hadn't heard of Ed back in the Midwest but I was good at cleaning toilets, finished all my campground loops by lunch and snuck into the meadows, filled with buffalo dung, surrounded by griz-scratched lodgepole . . . and lay in the sun, harvesting straw-berries and huckleberries, reading Abbey.

Evenings I joined the softball team, the Canyon Clowns, also known as the Raven Idiots. Specialists at hitting dou-bles, since that's where we tapped the keg. Sound a nasal caw caw anywhere in the Greater Yellowstone Ecosystem and you're likely to raise an alumnus. Stop into an art shop in Gardiner, do a little firefighting, crash your car in Grand Te-ton and let the EMT patch you up, release a few wolves in the Lamar Valley . . . anywhere, just sound off with a caw caw, or a more authentic k-gnaw k-gnaw, and you'll raise a know-ing smile.

Soon I was wrenching with the monkeys. Minor stuff, mainly. A little antidevelopment work. Most of the wrench-ing dedicated to pleasure. The Raven Idiots, sneaking into hot-pots for midnight baths. Running from the road rangers weighted down with badges and guns.

Too soon the elk began bugling. Griz tearing up a hillside for ground squirrels. COB on my first season. A chance for fame. A chance to COB my seasonal career forever. The low-power radio station was locked in a closet on my loop of toi-lets. The grizzly bear warning, an 8-track broadcasting over and over, to all the RVs. Don't feed the bears. Beware, the bears will eat you. I unlocked the door. Had a tape of Wood-stock. Jimi Hendrix. Over and over, Oh say can you see . . . a warning against RVs.

Chickened out.

Twelve seasons later, with a few seasons off to work year-round in the real world, and I'm wondering, remembering Ed, if it's better to bite the hand that feeds you. Or to gnaw it a little, season after season.

Cleaner of toilets. Then backcountry ranger. Fire lookout for the Forest Service, a few miles north of Mexico. Back to the Park Service ... supervisory ranger of a fire crew in a wilderness above Tucson. Bio-tech on the same mountain, studying the ecological benefits of wildfire. These last four seasons at Grand Teton as a fire monitor, a manager and proselytizer for natural fire.

Park Service acronyms this park as GRTE. We call it Gertie, or Gritty. We call it home, home until the elk bugle in the meadows, and the coyotes howl. Moose and black bears wander through our front yards. Sandhill cranes fly their waving snake-necks down Cottonwood Creek, ka-ronk, ka-ronk, and we pack our cars and trucks. COB to Gertie. But returning, season after season. Burt, the Oklahoma Cherokee who lives next door, coming back for seventeen seasons, some of the climbing rangers for longer. Average tenure for the permanent rangers, the bureaucratically ambitious ones, might be three, maybe four years tops.

In wintertime I write and teach, sometimes environmental writing. Always teaching that writing must be an ethical and concerned act—and, above all, not a boring act. As I learned from Ed.

Travel the West, work as a ranger, do a little writing, and people will nod, smile. "Like Abbey," they say. Sometimes they nod and curse. I nod back. "Maybe a little," I say. A little like Ed, a bit of hell-raising, a tad of gumption, standing up for the land. Sometimes, if it's a ranger nodding and smiling,

I'll add that Ed was my teacher, and the ranger will smile even bigger. Ed was real, after all. Not just some myth. And it's that smile, those many smiles, that remind me: Abbey lives. Lives on among the tradition of wild and independent and land-loving rangers, a tradition launched by Thoreau, the prototypical seasonal, carried on by Muir and John Van Dyke. The swashbuckling Teddy Roosevelt grabs the land for all of us and Mary Austen teaches us to worship it. Add a government salary and you get Aldo Leopold. Cut the salary a little, add a revolution and a sense of humor, and you get Ed.

Abbey's a hard act to follow. But he's being followed, expanded, debated. A new generation of Western writers live with Ed as a mentor or tormentor. But as many words as Ed inspires, he also inspires action. And that inspiration lives on. Wander the West and you'll hear the spoken stories of Ed, still alive. Like a grizzly's footstep, so heavy in the mud that it dries deep, lasts for months.

He was sick, says my friend Katherine. Had a bad stomach, way out on the North Rim, so I drove him in his truck, hundreds of miles, and all the way we listened to these great classical tapes, like the flute was taking us back to civilization.

Cocky bastard, says a scrawny man from Globe, Arizona, who worked as Ed's relief lookout—but most relief lookouts aren't as suited to solitude as the main lookout, nor as attuned to the need to communicate, sometimes in foul language and mood, after ten days alone. And this relief lookout was squirrelier than most.

I was walking alone in the canyon, a ranger says, when I heard this great Kokopelli flute, like I was being haunted . . . and it was Abbey, up on a rock.

Never there when we had a fire, says a ranger from the North Rim. But he had all these women visiting.

And so on.

Working my way through grad school, driving south of town to write for a quality little newspaper in a retirement community backed by open-pit mines, the Santa Rita mountains, and cattle-gnawed desert. I covered county government and real estate scams, plus thought pieces, since I was a grad student. My editor assigns me the big bicentennial party for the First Amendment. Sponsored by the local ACLU chapter. Speakers to include Ed Abbey. He and I had already drunk a few cups of coffee at the Student Union, stewing over our contradictory addictions to newspapers and wilderness. The news of yesterday versus the news of all yesterday's evolution, the news of sun and rain, wind and erosion and ecological adaptation. And now I was to be Ed's reporter.

At the Art Museum, ties and cocktail dresses and cocktails, everyone wealthy enough to support the First Amendment, back-slapping self-congratulations, plus a good speech on banned books by another of my professors, the writer Bob Houston. Ed takes the podium, and he says, yes, a great amendment, his favorite, but once you sign on with the First you have to support all speech ... *Hustler* included. And while we're talking about amendments, how about that Second Amendment: no freedom of speech without the weapons to back it up, and so on, the PC crowd squirming, before anybody knew what PC was.

Ed always asked us to question our assumptions. To argue for what you believe. To stand for something so fiercely that your beliefs will survive his absurd and logical (if one-sided) questions.

That's what my wife Zita thinks, who, as a literary critic, has a bit more distance on Abbey. Her thesis: Abbey's work, his life, the political and aesthetic movements that he helped launch, taken together, have given us a place to stand in. What you stand for must grow from the place you've chosen to stand on. My wife paraphrasing my professor. Me paraphrasing my wife. Each of whom has helped me find a place to stand.

Recently Zita reread all Abbey's work for an encyclopedia article. Sometimes, when Abbey's tone, or the maleness of his logic, began to annoy her, she would remember a quote of his: "We're none of us good enough for the world we live in." A quote I repeat back to her, when I begin to annoy.

To which I sometimes add the park ranger's corollary: We may not be good enough, but we're damn well going to live in this world.

Camus says it better: "Poverty prevented me from judging that all was well under the sun and in history; the sun taught me that history was not all."

And Wendell Berry teaches it best. In a workshop on environmental writing, Berry looked at the intro paragraph of a dozen nature essays by us budding nature writers. And he asked: "Where does this take place? Where is the place?"

The place I stand? COB on the thirteenth season in the Park Service. I'm cleaning the toilet in my seasonal cabin, preparing for final checkout. On the local real estate market, my view of the Tetons is literally worth $1 million. Or more. My cabin, once part of the Highlands dude ranch, is lodged between the sagebrush flats and Cottonwood Creek. Sometimes I walk the quarter mile to Timbered Island where plastic flowers decorate the grave of an old resident. More often I walk upcreek to Geraldine's Rock, grave of the second woman to climb Grand Teton ("It means the Big Boo-som," my five-year-old daughter explains to my mother), and to Fabian's Cabin, Geraldine's home and then home to the lawyer who secretly bought all the dude ranches for Rockefeller, who then donated the land to the Park Service.

Where do I stand? I stand in a park and also I stand in the Park Service, protector of our nation's natural and cultural wonders. The NPS mission brings tourist dollars to the West by providing clean toilets to the millions who come to pet the tame elk and buffalo. The Park Service also fights for a budget that barely mentions science and research. Yet the land, the land and the park rangers that this land inspires, and the backpackers, wolf-worshippers, fisher-people, hikers. . . . This land transforms you.

Of course, its sublimity, part transcendent, part terrifying, can also numb your soul. Which is why we need Ed. Bare-souled. Rough-edged. Unforgiving of the tramplers of the land, be they tourists or bureaucrats.

Does the Park Service have a conscience? More than most bureaucracies, less than your average poodle. Do the Park Service's workers—the rangers and biologists and firefighters and maintenance folk and interpreters—have an ethic? Mostly. Like the backcountry supervisor who questions the necessity and aesthetics of overflights to satellite-track wildlife. Like all manner of rangers—climbing rangers, road rangers, EMTs, helitack rangers—who routinely risk their lives to save injured tourists. Like the interpreters who sneak controversial environmental messages into their nightly slide shows.

All bureaucracies serve their budget first. Then their culture. Finally their mission. To protect the land: if that is your job, you owe a bit of your backbone to Abbey comma Edward. Ranger comma seasonal. The Park Service direct-deposits my wages to the Bank of Jackson Hole, but it is the land that direct-deposits into my soul, my spirit. It's the land we owe, not the bureaucracy.

That was Ed's message. The elk are bugling, as are the rangers, and I say COB, Ed. Till next season.

CHILTON WILLIAMSON, JR.

Abbey Lives!

Fifteen years after I arrived in the West, I can no longer recall
how I first became aware of Edward Abbey, though I do know
that I had been the book editor of a national magazine for
nearly four years before the name penetrated my consciousness. (The parochialism of the New York literati.) But I remember as if it were yesterday buying an armload of his
books at the Zion Bookstore in Salt Lake City (capital of the
only society on earth where a Jew is a gentile) and reading
them in bed in my single-bedroom rental in the Regency
Apartments in Kemmerer while blizzards raged out-of-
doors and an occasional pistol discharged in one of the surrounding units, followed by drunken shouts and a confused
roaring. I was working in the oil patch that winter, arriving
home at odd hours of the day and night, my biological clock
gone haywire, my muscles aching, my body stiff from the
forty- and fifty-below zero temperatures; and though I accomplished little reading in those months, I did manage to
plough through everything of Abbey's I could find in Salt
Lake. Quite an effort—like managing to drink a case of beer
after being lost in the desert all day. He has been dead nearly
six years now, still owing me the protracted horseback trip
along the Mexican border we had promised one another, but,
as if by some miracle, the books have started coming again:

Confessions of a Barbarian: Selections from the Journals of Edward Abbey, 1951–1989 (Boston: Little, Brown, 1994), edited and with an introduction by David Petersen, this fall and, next year, a volume of his letters, also edited by Petersen, a long-time friend. And of several biographies rumored to be in the making, the first—not really a biography—has recently been published: *Epitaph for a Desert Anarchist: The Life and Legacy of Edward Abbey* (New York: Atheneum, 1994), by James Bishop, Jr.

Was Abbey really a barbarian—in the pejorative rather than the classical sense of the term—and an anarchist? By the standard of Bill Clinton and Al Gore, who exhort us plaintively to have "faith in government," he certainly was the latter, while what Chesterton called "the huge and healthy sadness" of the pre-Christian era pervades *Confessions*. According to the vulgar and narrow understanding of his day, Ed Abbey was politically unclassifiable, a torpedo launched at those ungainly iron Liberty Ships of carefully welded opinion. Believing that the writer unprepared to tell the truth had better be looking around for something else to do, he did not strive for approbation or awards ("prizes," he wrote to Irving Howe, who had just offered him an award from the American Academy and Institute of Arts and Letters, "are for little boys"). And to the present Age of Sensitivity, he was anathema: tender, over-sensitized, and insecure souls could either toss the insult back, or grow a thicker skin—or suffer. In the company I mostly keep, the name Edward Abbey is either unrecognized or despised. Those of my friends (cattle ranchers, miners, oilfield roughnecks, local business people) who are familiar with the legend but have neither read nor heard of the highly disruptive speech Abbey delivered at the University of Montana in Missoula in 1985 against a background of shouts and jeers and gunfire in the parking lot, would probably be able to guess correctly the gist of his remarks. ("I'm in favor of putting the public lands livestock grazers out of business. . . . Almost anywhere and everywhere you go in the American West you find hordes of these ugly, clumsy, stupid, bawling, stinking, fly-covered, shit-smeared, disease-spreading brutes. . . . I've never heard of a coyote as dumb as a sheepman. . . . The cowboy is . . . a farm boy in leather britches and a comical hat. . . . Anytime you go into a small Western town, you'll find [the ranchers] at the nearest drugstore, sitting around all morning drinking coffee, talking about their tax breaks.") Among my first reactions to Abbey's work was the thought that the author insufficiently appreciated the degree to which the physical and social openness of the West depends upon the ranching "industry," as the Western ranch is unimaginable outside the context of the wilderness surrounding it—a fact of which the present generation of ranchers needs to be reminded. Yet, of Abbey's eight novels, one (*The Brave Cowboy*) has for its hero a farm boy in britches, while another (*Fire on the Mountain*) is the story of an elderly rancher who defies the attempts of the federal government to condemn his property for a missile range. More than he scorned Western cattle growers as "welfare parasites" and despoilers of the land, Abbey admired the best of them for their independence, their toughness, and their stubborn commitment to the preindustrial values held by citizens of the old American Republic whose passing he deplored and lamented.

An American original and individualist who resisted mass opinion all his life, Abbey in late career suffered the inexorable fate of the celebrated nonconformist by inadvertently helping to create and shape it. In some degree he had himself to blame, since he chose against dissociating or distancing himself from the environmental groupies and monkey-wrench cultists who fawned on him. But James Bishop, though inept in his role of literary critic, is sensitive to the importance of his subject as a social critic as well as a "nature writer" and environmentalist. Abbey's true subject, he suggests (echoing an essay by Wendell Berry), was himself—a self that could not be complete in a world despoiled by a self-ravaged society. "True human freedom," Abbey remarked a year before his death, "economic freedom, political freedom, social freedom, remain basically linked to physical freedom, sufficient space, enough land." Unlike the majority of "environmentalists," he believed that what is finally at stake is not the future of the earth, which will endure for eons after human beings, their worst accomplished, have driven themselves to extinction, but that of humanity and the civilization it has created—especially in America. As Bishop points out, Abbey's interest was not in saving the world (which he regarded as unsalvageable, sordid, and barbaric) but in saving *America*, a special land inhabited by the chosen people who had created for themselves the Constitution and the Bill of Rights. It was this interest, as much as the vision of the vast and multisplendored Western landscape being overrun by tens or scores of millions of Latin Americans, that prompted his notorious ("racist," "xenophobic") stand against immigration from the Third World. "How many of us, truthfully, would *prefer* to be submerged in the Latin-Caribbean version of civilization? . . . Harsh words, but somebody has to say them."

Had Henry David Thoreau's view of the Mexican-American War carried the day, Abbey's Road would have been patrolled by the *federales*. Still, Thoreau was a hero for Abbey, the man to whose work his own has most often been compared. In fact, it is much better than that, *Walden* having all the natural interest of a walk in Central Park, enlivened by transcendentalist musings in lieu of a few good muggings. Abbey deserves to be treated much more broadly as a late twentieth-century representative of a long and distinguished line of American antiurban intellectuals, many of whom also opposed social, economic, and technological giantism and the centralization of the state, that includes Jefferson, Melville, Hawthorne, Poe, Josiah Royce, Lewis Mumford—*and* Thoreau. Abbey's prose, for all its revolutionary mystique, has many sober and even polite antecedents. A passage from Royce's *Race Questions, Provincialism and Other American Problems* (1908), expounding the Harvard philosopher's "higher provincialism," has the Abbey ring to it:

> There [to the province] must we flee from the stress of the now too vast and problematic life of the nation as a whole. . . . [N]ot in the sense of a cowardly and permanent retirement, but in the sense of a search for renewed strength, for a social inspiration, for the salvation of the individual from the overwhelming forces of consolidation. Freedom . . . dwells now in the small social group, and has its securest home in the provincial life. The nation by itself, apart from the influence of the province, is in danger of becoming an incomprehensible monster, in whose presence the individual loses his right, his self-consciousness, and his dignity.

Those over-consistent souls who remark that as Thoreau's cabin was within walking distance of his mother's house and her washboard, so Abbey's primary residence over the years was the sprawling ultramodern city of Tucson have missed the point. For Abbey, the American West—"All of it"—was his province, defined not only in terms of wilderness but of its (ever-decreasing) remoteness from the Eastern monster that the West seemed bent on recreating between the Front Range and the Pacific Ocean. To Thoreau's statement that, "What we call wilderness is a civilization other than our own," Abbey might have added, "What I call civilization is surrounded by a civilization other than our own."

Confessions reveals a susceptibility to the conviviality of city life and even to the aesthetics of the cityscape (though characteristically Abbey preferred Hoboken, where he spent several years while married to one of his two Jewish wives, to Manhattan) but none at all to small-town or farm life which he, having been raised on a farm in western Pennsylvania, loathed. For Abbey, happiness was always one thing or the other, megalopolis or wilderness: an unexceptionable preference that nevertheless compromised his appreciation of rural culture and, especially, agriculture.

That, for several reasons, is too bad. For one thing, it left him vulnerable to the ideological excesses of the Social Democratic Wilderness Party, including its Deep Ecology faction, and therefore to plausible counterattack by the Enemy. (What right anyway have city people and suburbanites—at least 90 percent of environmentalists in America—to create policy for the management of wilderness and other rural lands, of which their knowledge is almost entirely theoretical and secondhand? The land, as Latin American revolutionaries say, belongs to those who work it. Imagine the uproar if the farmers of upstate New York insisted on writing crime control bills for New York City!) Another is that it prevented him from recognizing that the maintenance of a rural culture based on ranching is infinitely more important to the preservation of the Western United States than any number of wilderness set-asides engineered by congressional representatives from urban California and bluestocking districts on Manhattan Island. The third is that it blinkered and blinded him against a truth that seemed axiomatic to human beings throughout most of their history, and that is being rediscovered today even as it is most emphatically denied.

"The main problem of the coming century," John Lukacs says, "will be people's relationship to the land. But the pollution of land, indeed of all matter, is preceded and produced by the pollution of minds." Early in the twentieth century if not before, the causal connection between man's depredation of the natural world and his own self-degradation began to be noticed. Romano Guardini concluded that culture arises from a living human relationship with nature, an argument that was developed in the United States over the next decade by the Southern Agrarians; Santayana in his last book published in 1953 wrote that an animal economy, based on the breeding and hunting of animals, is the natural condition of man: neither wilderness nor city but *rus in urbe* or *urbs ruri*, the rural center. What Lukacs calls the "insubstantialization of matter"—its remoteness from our lives in combination with the increasing "abstractness of patterns of thought"— in his opinion demands "a conscious realization, not only of the sinful nature of man, but the already overdue necessity to rethink the entire meaning of progress," an agendum that Abbey pressed for forty years.

"Lavender cumuli floating like armadas of men-o'-war over the arid canyons, bombarding them with lightning bolts; hisses and shouts of wind; the irritable whining of flies; clear open seas of blue and green to the west and north; the charged stillness, the heat, the sudden flurry of the whirlwind; . . . danger, pressure, tension, anticipation in the air. . . ." Despite a somewhat messy and disordered life that included five marriages and in which satyriasis yielded only to ill health and premature death, there is nothing of the barbarian in the man who could create this description of afternoon storms above the summer desert of southeastern Utah. Nothing, that is, except the alien, the dissenter from a society widely considered superior to his own.

Meeting Ed Abbey

I first met Ed Abbey in Salt Lake City. We'd each been invited separately to the University of Utah to speak. He was kind enough to ask if I'd like to join him, to merge our dates in a benefit reading for the Utah Wilderness Association. I told him I'd be honored.

The hours before the reading were chaotic. Each of us spoke to separate groups of people. We lunched and then dined with faculty and students. We didn't have a chance to talk for more than a few minutes. But my impression of him hardly changed after that. He seemed both serene and startled in our moments together. There was something vital in him. I liked him immediately.

Writers, of course, are exceedingly diverse, and perhaps more wary around each other on first meeting than most, when they are put together by someone else in a public situation. The public persona each maintains to protect his privacy can make a wall between them, and distort what they might otherwise easily share. Too, one writer might believe the other is simply a drummer of some kind, and no writer.

The first words Ed and I had that night were about privacy. We were eating dinner. I said something about the vulnerability a reader can exhibit in a letter, and how respectful and careful I thought you had to be with such feelings. I was looking for a point of agreement. There is little enough time in life given to any of us; if your work is essentially private, it is better to locate the floor of an honest friendship quickly than to either proselytize or cajole with someone newly met, to assume agreements are there which are not. Writers, in my experience, can be courteous toward each other to a fault, especially in private; but they inhabit different and private universes, and the will to remain in them is iron. No friendship persists that requires one or the other to always defer, or which does not continue on a basis of mutual regard.

Readers bring writers together in curious ways. To some extent, writers are the creations of the shorthanded imagery of newspapers, of literary gossip. They are grouped regionally, placed in various "schools," or presumed to be somewhat like each other because they write about similar things. But writers maintain only tenuous friendships on these grounds—or become estranged because someone of note has glibly put them together, or separated them. Writers do not become friends solely because they write about the same things, nor solely because they admire each other's prose. They have to like each other as people, often as the people readers rarely know, because no writer can stand that kind of intimacy with readers and go on writing.

Ed was about to take a bite of his dinner when I said I thought you had to be respectful of vulnerability in readers. He paused with his fork in the air, and said yes, from somewhere far away in himself. The two of us, private men, both somewhat shy, found ourselves looking silently into the same abyss, and acknowledging a similar vulnerability in ourselves. A cynical remark at that moment and we would have forever gone our separate ways. But there was none. It was a moment of trust.

Writers, especially when they are possessed of some

strong sense of their own worth and work—which is not always—are inclined compassionately toward each other. Each knows the other has struggled to make sense of that vast interior landscape of impressions, overheard conversations, sensual memories, feelings of longing and anguish, remembered sentences, and that wilderness of ethical rage and hope that creates literature. Only discipline and an abiding hunger produce fine work. And if another writer has produced fine work—you may not be stunned by its language, or agree with its sentiment, or even be keenly interested in its subject—you are moved. You know he has vanquished a nameless creature, a dreary beast that breaks tenacity, undermines faith, and leaves in its wake a convoluted prose. You know the same animal.

In those first moments with Ed I was struck by what I admire most in anyone: honesty; unpretentious convictions; a bedrock opposition to what menaces life. I imagined we might share enemies, though I felt no inclination to enumerate or describe them.

We read that evening together. The stories we read, about men and women in unmanipulated Western landscapes, expressed sentiments closely shared with people in the audience. I felt that night, strongly, almost physically, the beliefs I have about language—its power to evoke life and to remove pain—and the obligation writers have to dismantle the false notion of their own prophesies, the unexamined prejudices that can compel a public figure to demagoguery. I spoke that evening of a Spanish concept—*querencia*, a common, defended ground, an emotional landscape shared by listener and storyteller. Its defense implies a threat; without threat, without menace, there is neither literature nor heroism.

Abbey, with his caustic accusations and droll humor, his Western skepticism, was an encouragement to stand up for belief. As I listened to him read, I thought, well, here is a good man, a fine and decent neighbor. He reads before university audiences like this, is misunderstood, misquoted, misappropriated, but he goes on writing—an endless penetration of his own mind, a hunger for greater clarity, precision. How better this than were he to turn to politics, or to take solemnly the notion that he speaks for anyone but himself.

Since that evening I have gotten to know Ed better. The large and slow pleasure he takes in looking over the contours of a landscape, his affinity for music. A characteristic broad, sudden, and uncalculated smile. His ingenuous shyness, so at odds with the public image of a bold iconoclast.

We have specific disagreements, he and I, which we do not pursue, out of courtesy and a simple awareness of the frailty of human life, the gulf between human intent and human act. But nothing much has changed between us since that night, except that we have grown closer out of mutual regard, some unspoken sense of an opposition to a threat, a definition of which we largely agree upon.

You can point to the quirks and miscalculations of any writer exposed to the searing heat of public acclaim. Better to select what is admirable and encouraging, if a man is not a charlatan. Abbey's self-effacing honesty, the ease with which he can admire someone else's work without feeling he diminishes his own—these are qualities wonderful to find in any human. How fortunate for all of us that they are found in a man widely known and well regarded, who persists in writing out his understanding of the world as though it mattered to more than only himself.

RICHARD SHELTON

Creeping Up on *Desert Solitaire*

I.

Edward Abbey's *Desert Solitaire* has been hailed by critics as "an underground classic." Does this mean that the book was prematurely buried and will never rise from the grave? It seems an odd way to describe a book so filled with sky and sun, endless vistas, and soaring birds. In fact, *Desert Solitaire* is about the least "underground" book I have ever read. But it might be a "classic," whatever that is. Many literary "classics" have been hailed in the past, only to be lost sight of by the next generation of readers. Perhaps these books went underground, to the place, it would seem, where *Desert Solitaire* was born.

At any rate, few books in modern times can legitimately be called "classics" because few survive from one generation of readers to the next. And the term is becoming increasingly meaningless since we live in a time when we are not even sure there will be a next generation. And if there is a next generation which grows to maturity, will its members be readers in our sense of the word, or will they deal only with computerese and images on a television screen?

We know from medical statistics that a large percentage of the present generation of beautiful young people will be at least partially deaf and partially crippled by the time they reach middle age, one affliction caused by a penchant for extremely loud noise called "music," and the other by the current fad for jogging, which ultimately damages knees and ankles. What will these poor deaf cripples do when they are middle-aged, since their hearing impairments will limit the pleasure of television and they won't be able to move about much on their damaged legs? Perhaps they will revive reading as a pastime. Perhaps they will dig up old "underground classics" and read them. It might become a fad, and they could do worse.

But what will they think of Edward Abbey's *Desert Solitaire* when they finally get it exhumed? Lord, I don't know, and I don't want to know. The only way I can approach such a contemporary book critically is to creep up on it from behind, from the past into which it is rapidly receding. I cannot suggest that it will survive beyond the present generation of readers any more than I can suggest that the deserts and other beautiful places in this country will survive the forces of progress and tourism. I can hope, but hope is cheap and there is little of it in *Desert Solitaire*. Nor is it the stuff of serious literary criticism.

II.

"Serious critics, serious librarians, serious associate professors of English will if they read this work dislike it intensely; at least I hope so," says Abbey in his "Author's Introduction" to *Desert Solitaire*. I was an associate professor of English when I first read *Desert Solitaire* and, with the exception of this patronizing sentence, I liked it intensely. In fact, we associate professor types ate it up, as did our fusty friends the librarians. And it is a matter of record that most of the critics gave it high praise. Perhaps none of us were "serious" enough. But we have been loyal in praising the book and recommending it to everyone. Some of us have even taught it in our literature classes, heaven forbid! And Abbey, who is now a lecturer of English himself, does not seem to have been too displeased with our response to the book. Looking back, his statement seems to be part of a romantic "young rebel" pose based upon faulty assumptions and generalizations. But perhaps it was not merely a pose. Perhaps Abbey was trying to hide his love letters behind a smoke screen of abrasive rhetoric.

Obviously he wanted the book to be abrasive and controversial. At times he thunders like an Old Testament prophet denouncing the sins of a doomed people. At times he turns to ridicule with the flair, if not the subtlety, of an eighteenth-century satirist. But somehow or other those parts of the book went over our heads. As a matter of fact, we didn't use our heads much at all when we read *Desert Solitaire*. We fell in love with it. We took it directly into our hearts, however unused those desiccated organs were to such reactions. It became known as a sensuous, romantic masterpiece—exactly what its author, presumably, did not want it to be. Late in the book Abbey refers to "that gallant infirmity of the soul called romance—that illness, that disease, the insidious malignancy which must be chopped out of the heart once and for all, ground up, cooked, burnt to ashes . . . consumed."

Desert Solitaire was written by an arch-romantic trying desperately not to be romantic. But between the realist who sees the hopeless condition of contemporary society with its hideous impact on nature and the lyric lover who wants only to sing about the beauties of the natural world "falls the shadow," as Mr. Eliot said; and Mr. Eliot had similar problems himself. That shadow is an unresolvable tension, the hope of the hopelessly romantic impulse faced with the inevitability of disaster. Out of such tension comes art, and perhaps without it there can be no art. This battle between two opposing impulses gives the book tension, drama, the shock of the real, and saves it from being just another memoir. Much of *Desert Solitaire* is a love lyric. But each time the lover gives in to romantic outpourings, the realist asserts himself, kills a rabbit or denounces, categorically, the shallowness, greed, and hypocrisy of man.

A reviewer for the *New York Times* called the book "a ride on a bucking bronco," and I can see what he means but would quarrel, somewhat, with the analogy. It is true that the book is all up and down, but the distances Abbey covers in both directions are infinitely greater than those experienced by anyone on a bucking horse. Stylistically and aesthetically the book rises to grand peaks of romantic beauty only to plunge suddenly downward with terrifying speed. And this pattern is often reflected in the physical actions described. Abbey is always climbing mountains or going to high places where his romantic spirit is nourished by the immensity of space and distance. Then he descends precipitously, almost in panic, from the place of too much beauty. He climbs Mt. Tukuhnikivats, the "island in the desert," grows lyrical at its summit, and then descends at a "sensational clip" by riding a slab of stone down the abrupt, snow-covered side of the mountain.

But he likes best to stand on the edge of a cliff or at the summit of a very high place and watch the birds, often buzzards, soaring without effort through the sea of space below. The descent beckons. He feels the lure of high places and the desire to launch himself into space like Rilke looking out from the balcony of a romantic castle tower above the Rhine.

He even quotes Rilke with respect and then, with that sudden turning away from the romantic, describes him as "a German poet who lived off countesses." In the chapter called "The Dead Man at Grandview Point" Abbey creates a symbol of the earthbound, pedestrian man who allows himself to die of thirst and exposure at the edge of a cliff rather than take the romantic plunge, after which his body would become part of the soaring birds rather than a stinking mess of putrefaction zipped up in a rubber bag, a burden for those who must carry it miles toward a waiting ambulance and further indignities.

One of the results of this tension, this attraction of opposites—the soaring romantic and the cynically realistic, high places and the sudden descent—is that Abbey, as he portrays himself in the book, is a round and believable character. No character in any of his novels has the depth, the believability, the absolute feel of a real person that Ed Abbey in *Desert Solitaire* has. Compared to Ed Abbey in *Desert Solitaire*, *The Brave Cowboy* or anybody in *The Monkey Wrench Gang* or *Good News* is flat and dimensionless. But this man, this Ed Abbey who can fall in love with a weathered juniper and then coolly consider beating a companion's brains out with a beer bottle, this man is real.

At times he is complex, deep, philosophical, and wise. At other times he is shallow, cynical, or cruel; and he visits most of the way stations between. Whether he is the Edward Abbey who wrote the book or that Edward Abbey's view of himself or a purely fictional creation is a matter of little importance, except perhaps to the youthful members of the cult which has grown up around the book, those who are sometimes puzzled and possibly a bit disappointed by the tall, soft-spoken, shy, and reticent man named Edward Abbey whom they travel hundreds of miles to meet.

Whoever he is, the Ed Abbey in *Desert Solitaire* is human, and he works. He works the way a character in fiction should work. He has weight, stature, variety. He poses and postures, makes fun of himself and others, takes himself seriously, is loving and hateful, strong and weak by turns. And he is created right on the spot, full-blown, with almost no anterior personality and only the most minimal explanation as to how he got there or how he got to be who he is.

In the "Author's Introduction" Abbey tells the reader that he spent three summers as a park ranger at Arches National Monument in southeast Utah. The "Author's Introduction" is brief, and much of what it says deals with the National Park Service and with Abbey's method of writing the book. He says, ". . . most of the substance of this book is drawn, sometimes direct and unchanged, from the pages of journals I kept. . . ." If the date and place of its signing can be trusted, the "Author's Introduction" was written in Nelson's Marine Bar in Hoboken in April, 1967, after the book was completed. But it does not seem to have been written by the Ed Abbey who is the narrator and point-of-view character in the book. That Ed Abbey appears quite suddenly on page one. The first thing he says is, "This is the most beautiful place on earth." And he's not referring to Nelson's Marine Bar in Hoboken.

The line between fiction and nonfiction, between storytelling and reportage or writing essays, has always been tenuous. If it seems to be growing more tenuous lately with the nonficiton novels of Truman Capote and Norman Mailer, that is only because we have a shortsighted view. There was once a Daniel Defoe, and before him a Thomas Nash, a Robert Greene, and others. We have come to accept the principle that novelists make up stories and writers of nonfiction do not, but that is a recent convention and will not hold up to

historical facts. It seems to me that if the literary output of
Edward Abbey, as a whole, should be compared to that of
some illustrious writer of the past, that writer would probably be Daniel Defoe. I am not prepared to pursue this and
feel intimidated even by bringing it up, but perhaps someone
better equipped to do so might want to consider it at length.

Certainly some sections of *Desert Solitaire* are short
stories, some are tales, some are vignettes, some are narrative
reports based on journal notes. In some sections the author
treats plot, character, and dialogue exactly as a short story
writer would treat them. In other sections he uses the essayist's means to convince the reader in regard to philosophical
issues.

What holds these disparate structural elements together?
Perhaps it is not even legitimate to ask such a question this
late in the twentieth century. Perhaps unity or structural in-
tegrity is no longer an element we can expect in a book. But
I feel a strong, almost desperate, attempt on the author's part
to make this book hang together, to make it a unit rather than
a hodgepodge of essays, narratives, and short stories. And for
me he succeeds, although if I had been given an outline of
the book before it was written, I would probably have said it
couldn't be done. But *Desert Solitaire* is a *tour de force*, and
such works, by definition, must succeed in spite of severe
technical obstacles.

Since there is little unity of subject or structure, Abbey
tries to rely on the unities of time and place to make the book
cohere. He compresses the events of three seasons in the wilderness into one season, and he generally limits himself to a
loosely defined geographical area, although that area is quite
literally as big as all outdoors. Sometimes he violates one or
both of these limitations, narrating events which took place
at an earlier period or in a somewhat different place, such as
the story of the ill-fated uranium prospector Albert T. Husk

or the account of Abbey's sojourn in Havasu Canyon. But the stories are fascinating, and most readers are not all that familiar with the geography anyway. After all, it is a remote area in a godforsaken corner of Utah.

There are, however, several things which recur in the book much like *leitmotifs*. Somehow, we are more accustomed to such devices in poetry or the novel, and it is easy to miss their structural and unifying functions in a work of nonfiction. The lone juniper, the red bandana, the trailer, the natural stone terrace, the outdoor fire—to these Abbey returns the reader again and again. They define a space which is the center of the book, the place where Abbey sleeps, eats, and meditates on the desert. Near the center of that space is the fire, a small circle of light which gives the book a *locus* around which to circulate.

It would seem easy to say that *Desert Solitaire* has a unity of subject because, as its name implies, it is a book about the desert; and there might be some truth in this, but it is also misleading. There are many books which we would all agree were written about the desert, but they were written by scientists like Paul Griswold Howes, Forrest Shreve, or William McGinnies, or by historians like Eugene Hollow. Some of these are fairly heavy going for a nonspecialist, but they are clearly *about* the desert. Others, easier to read but still filled with factual information, were written by amateur naturalists like Joseph Wood Krutch. Is *Desert Solitaire* about the desert?

We need not quibble over this. Let us go straight to the horse's mouth, keeping in mind that even the horse can sometimes be wrong or misleading. In his "Author's Introduction" Abbey says:

> This is not primarily a book about the desert. In recording
> my impressions of the natural scene I have striven above all

for accuracy, since I believe that there is a kind of poetry, even a kind of truth, in simple fact. But the desert is a vast world, an oceanic world, as deep in its way and complex and various as the sea. Language makes a mighty loose net with which to go fishing for simple facts, when facts are infinite. . . . What I have tried to do then is something a bit different. Since you cannot get the desert into a book any more than a fisherman can haul up the sea with his nets, I have tried to create a world of words in which the desert figures more as medium than as material. Not imitation but evocation has been the goal.

I am primarily interested in three words here: "impressions," "medium," and "evocation." This could be the language of an impressionist painter or of a romantic poet. Yet the book is obviously neither a painting nor a poem. If the desert is a "medium" for something, what is it a "medium" for? And if "evocation" is Abbey's goal, what is he trying to evoke? There may not be definitive answers to these questions, but they are important questions nonetheless, since they lead to a central issue. If *Desert Solitaire* is not primarily about the desert, what is it about? And does it have any clear literary antecedents or models, or is it merely a twentieth-century anomaly?

The fact that Abbey talks about the book in terms one might use to describe a poem is a little frightening. Is it written in that abomination called "poetic prose"? I certainly hope not, and a close look at the language assures me that it is not. Even at his most rhapsodic, and Abbey does rhapsodize from time to time, the language is crisp, muscular, idiomatic, and concrete. There is an orderliness and clarity about his prose which suggests French models. His writing is never muddy nor self-indulgent, and if he sometimes flirts with "purple passages," they are only faintly lilac. The lyrical quality of *Desert Solitaire* arises from what Abbey is saying rather than from the way he says it. It comes from his attitude toward what he is writing about.

As for literary models, toward the end of the book Abbey provides a brief, handy-dandy list of books written about or in response to the desert. All of them have at least interested him, and some of them might have influenced him. In some cases he mentions only authors, but it is obvious which books he is referring to, and a mixed bag it is.

It includes four books (by John Wesley Powell, Everett Ruess, Charles M. Doughty, and T. E. Lawrence) which fall clearly into the category of travel and exploration, as well as two books by Wallace Stegner, one a biography and one a history. It refers, but not by title, to some of the novels of Paul Bowles and William Eastlake. The remaining three books are collections of essays. They include a book of essays on the Sonoran Desert by Joseph Wood Krutch, and a collection by Mary Austin, whose interests ranged from natural history to anthropology. The remaining book is unclassifiable. It might be considered a travel book, but it isn't. It might be considered a collection of essays on natural history, but it isn't. It is John Charles Van Dyke's turn-of-the-century masterpiece, *The Desert*, which Abbey refers to as "an unjustly forgotten book."

Of all the books on Abbey's list, *The Desert* has the strongest claim of being the direct literary antecedent of that part of *Desert Solitaire* which is presented in essay form. In 1901, in his "Preface-Dedication" to *The Desert* Van Dyke said:

> The love of Nature is after all an acquired taste. One begins by admiring the Hudson-River landscape and ends by loving the desolation of Sahara. Just why or how the change would be difficult to explain. You cannot always dissect a taste or a passion. Nor can you pin Nature to a board and chart her

beauties with square and compasses. One can give his impression and but little more. Perhaps I can tell you something of what I have seen in these two years of wandering; but I shall never be able to tell you the grandeur of these mountains, nor the glory of the color that wraps the burning sands at their feet. We shoot arrows at the sun in vain; yet still we shoot.

If we compare this passage with the passage from Abbey's "Author's Introduction" previously quoted, it becomes apparent that the two men are saying remarkably similar things. And in spite of the differences in prose styles which reflect the styles of two different periods, both express themselves in remarkably similar ways. Both use the term "impression," and both turn to metaphor to express the impossibility of a factual approach to their subject. But what, exactly, is their subject? Abbey talks about hauling up the entire sea in a net, and Van Dyke describes what he is doing as shooting arrows at the sun. They are both evasive, and thereby hangs a tale.

III.

The Desert by John Charles Van Dyke is a remarkable book not only because of what it is, but also because of what it is not. Although it is filled with precise observations, it does not provide the reader with the kind of facts provided by Joseph Wood Krutch's *The Desert Year.* And it is not a travel book, although its author had surely traveled. He was a handsome, asthmatic, forty-two-year-old art critic and art historian who wandered through the desert of the southwestern United States and northwestern Mexico for more than two years, sometimes on horseback and sometimes on foot. The subtitle of his book is *Further Studies in Natural Appearances*, and Van Dyke claims that it is a careful record of what he observed during his wanderings. But one of the strange things about it is that Van Dyke almost never tells the reader where he was while making particular observations, and much of the time the reader has no idea which of three different deserts Van Dyke was looking at.

In spite of that, Van Dyke had a pair of the best-trained eyes of his generation. He had spent much of his life looking at paintings and writing about paintings, aesthetics, and theories of visual perception. He was also a professor of art history at Rutgers University, and he was in love with the desert. His high degree of perceptual training combined with his extreme emotional involvement resulted in a book which glows from within.

He organizes his observations thematically in chapters with such titles as "Light, Air, and Color" or "Illusions." He describes and analyzes with the precision of a scientist and even performs simple scientific experiments to obtain more accurate information, but he writes from the standpoint of a lover. The desert holds him; and it holds him in spite of ill health, danger, deprivation, loneliness, and depression. Caught in the tension between the impulses of a scientist or scholar and those of a lover, he tries desperately to express his obsession:

> . . . you shall never see elsewhere as here the sunset valleys swimming in a pink and lilac haze, the great mesas and plateaus fading into blue distance, the gorges and canyons banked full of purple shadow. . . . And wherever you go, by land or sea, you shall not forget what you saw not but rather felt—the desolation and the silence of the desert.

A comparison of specific passages in *The Desert* and *Desert Solitaire* would provide evidence of nothing as startling as literary "borrowing," but it would provide interesting results. It would show two men with the same obsession, both in love with the same landscape. That landscape is a hard mistress and not the mistress of their choice, but neither of them had a choice. They had significantly different backgrounds and are writing more than sixty years apart. Their prose styles are quite different, but their music is the same, as each tries to come to grips with his own feelings.

"What is the peculiar quality or character of the desert that distinguishes it, in spiritual appeal, from other forms of landscape?" Abbey asks, as if he believes he could really answer the question, although he knows Van Dyke has already tried to answer it and failed. Van Dyke's version was: "What is it that draws us to the boundless and fathomless? Why should the lovely things of the earth . . . appear trivial and insignificant when we come face to face with . . . the desert?"

When Abbey speaks of being "caught by this golden lure," I think we begin to see what both of these books are about, and why neither of them falls neatly into any literary category. These books compare to most books about the desert as the description of a beautiful woman written by her lover would compare to a description of the same woman written by her physician. The physician's description might be more accurate; but the lover's description would go well beyond the physical, would involve the emotional and spiritual, and would undoubtedly be colored by how the woman had treated him. Abbey says, "I am convinced now that the desert has no heart." He is speaking as a man in love, as Van Dyke spoke before him.

The account of Abbey's leave-taking of Arches National

Monument in *Desert Solitaire* could easily be the description of a man parting from a woman with whom he is deeply in love, a woman he does not think he will ever see again. To use an old cliché, but one for which no adequate substitute has yet been found, it is heartbreaking: the preparations for departure; the long, sensuous lingering over every physical detail of the beloved; the awkward and sentimental gestures; then the need to be gone quickly while he still has the strength; and finally, while he is being driven away and it is too late, the desperate looking back. It has been done before in literature, and perhaps it is a stock scene; but it has never been done before, not even by Van Dyke, with a desert.

Van Dyke, in his "Preface-Dedication" says: "The desert has gone a-begging for a word of praise these many years. It never had a sacred poet; it has in me only a lover." Earlier in the same paragraph he says, "And so my book is only an excuse for talking about the beautiful things in this desert world. . . ." And perhaps that is a good enough answer to the question of what both *Desert Solitaire* and *The Desert* are about. Neither writer needs much excuse to talk about the beauty of his beloved; nor, for that matter, do any of us. The French have a name for such a thing when it is a poem. They call it a *blazon*, a catalogue of the beauty of the beloved. But we have no such category in English prose, and therefore both books remain quite without category, not an entirely undesirable place for a literary work to be.

Both Van Dyke and Abbey, while they were in the desert, were aware of its numinous quality, of some spirit which it contains or embodies. Van Dyke speaks of the desert's "soul," and Abbey speaks of its "heart." Both were frustrated, but their attempts to find it led them far beyond what most writers have been able to achieve when dealing with the desert.

Their search led them into the realms of the mystic or transcendental. Van Dyke's attempt, since it involved longer periods of total isolation, more danger, solitude, and deprivation, was probably greater. As he admits in his unpublished Autobiography, it destroyed his health and led him to the brink of madness. In *The Desert* he says:

> Was there ever such stillness as that which rests upon the desert at night? Was there ever such a hush as that which steals from star to star across the firmament? You perhaps think to break that spell by raising your voice in a cry; but you will not do so again. The sound goes but a little way and then seems to come back to your ear with a suggestion of insanity about it.

And Abbey provides a daytime version of the same mystery:

> There is something about the desert that the human sensibility cannot assimilate, or has not so far been able to assimilate. Perhaps that is why it has scarcely been approached in poetry or fiction, music or painting. . . . Meanwhile, under the vulture-haunted sky, the desert waits—mesa, butte, canyon, reef, sink, ecarpment, pinnacle, maze, dry lake, sand dune and barren mountain—untouched by the human mind.

Since both Van Dyke and Abbey were in love with the desert, their books have another element in common—a plea for its protection. And because of what happened to much of the desert of the southwestern United States in the more than sixty years since Van Dyke wrote *The Desert*, Abbey's book is more bitter, more pessimistic, more despairing; and this in spite of the fact that Van Dyke refers to man as nature's "one great enemy," and says, "The desert should never be reclaimed." After he wrote that, Van Dyke lived to see much of the Colorado and Mojave deserts destroyed by reclamation projects, and he witnessed the disastrous attempt to divert part of the Colorado River which created the Salton Sea.

But he did not see the worst, the horrors of progress: the destruction of large portions of the Sonoran Desert by agriculture, desert cities spreading like cancer, the further rape of the Colorado River to provide power to air-condition the tract houses and shopping malls of Phoenix. Abbey writes with a full knowledge of these horrors, and if his irony sometimes turns to bitterness, his bitterness is justified by what he has seen.

Abbey's employment as a park ranger, even in so remote a place as Arches National Monument, put him in an excellent position to view the American middle class in its tourist phase, with its penchant for litter, conveniences, and the automobile. His description of the American tourist is savagely accurate. He pinpoints the automobile as the immediate cause of the destruction of the natural environments which are supposed to be protected by the National Park Service, and blames that organization for encouraging the destruction of the very thing it is supposed to be protecting.

Nor is Abbey always negative. He proposes specific methods for "carving some of the fat off the wide bottom of the American middle class," and he outlines in detail a very sensible method for saving our national parks while still making them available to the people. One has only to go to Arches or Mesa Verde or any of the other national parks or monuments today to see that the governmental forces which control them have paid not the slightest attention to what he said.

It is probably because of Abbey's stand on environmental issues that *Desert Solitaire* has been tagged an "*underground* classic." I object to the use of the term "underground," since it suggests somehow that the book is subversive and makes it easier to dismiss Abbey's ideas and recommendations. But I see nothing subversive about *Desert Solitaire*. Abbey's very specific suggestions are aimed at conserving, not destroying.

And if, when he makes them, his tone at times is somewhat strident and abrasive, beneath it I always hear the voice of a lover trying desperately to protect the thing he loves. It is a strong, clear voice. The pity is there are not more voices like it.

JAMES R. HEPWORTH

Canis Lupus Amorus Lunaticum

In mid-October 1994, five writers met at a long table in Currigan Exhibition Hall at the Rocky Mountain Book Festival in Denver to discuss a single question: "Ed Abbey: Why Did That S.O.B. Make Such a Difference?" The six scheduled panelists, as I recall, included the editors of this volume; Robert Michael Pyle, a cryptobiologist and writer from Grays River, Washington; Ellen Meloy, a backcountry ranger and river runner from Utah; Dave Petersen, Abbey's friend and editor; and the chair, Russell Martin, a Colorado writer, whom Abbey once referred to as a "lit cricket."

My partner, Greg McNamee, had canceled early by pleading the exigencies of his miserable freelance existence and received an excused absence by our panel's organizer, Marilyn Auer of *The Bloomsbury Review*. When I had called at the last minute from my home in Idaho to plead my own excuses, Marilyn's patience scurried away on little mice feet that left behind tracers of telephone static. As the official Secret Agent of *The Bloomsbury Review*, she roared, it is your sacred duty to be there—or else.

So I borrowed food money from my three small children, charged my plane fare to the English Department, and the next day kissed my wife and flew to Denver.

Perhaps sixty people showed up to listen and watch the little spectacle that unfolded. Terry Tempest Williams came in late, winked, and blew a kiss at me (or was it for Dave Petersen?). I could see Jim Carrier from the *Denver Post*, one of the few honest journalists left in America, taking out his pencil. I think some of the Indians might have been there: Chief Wilma Mankiller from the Cherokee tribe in Oklahoma, Sherman Alexie from Wellpinit—the usual suspects, exactly the sort of people I tend to respect but who flutter my jitters. I kept hearing Marilyn Auer's voice on the phone, "Oh, for Christ's sake. It's just a panel. In that crowd, you won't be able to get a word in sideways even if you want to say something." Introductions were making the rounds. I tried to concentrate on the question. It was a good question, and I even liked the way Marilyn had phrased it: "Why Did That Son of a Bitch Make Such a Difference?"

"Son of a bitch," I kept mumbling under my breath. I liked the phrase. It was a good phrase. Maybe even too good.

Abbey, the cur. The contemptible mongrel hillbilly. The hairy lone wolf, *Canis lupus amorus lunaticum*, the hellhound who refused to heel, the shadower of the nation's conscience. The pitbull flower-puppy. Howler, growler, shit-eater, trail-sniffer, pointer, bird dog. . . . My notepad began to fill up.

If I ever paid back the $27.16 I owed my kids and let them have a dog, I decided, it would have to be a female and they'd have to name it something more memorable than "Ed." But what if they disobeyed me? What if they did christen the pup "Ed"? And then in my mind I began to call the dog, "Here, Ed." I heard myself whispering, "He-eere, Ed. Come on, boy."

Almost at once something alien and peculiar and perfectly mundane happened. The door at the back of the room was still open where late-latecomers straggled in. The introductions had now moved even closer to me. Our chairman had already introduced himself. To his left sat Dave Petersen, who had also finished his preliminary, and to Martin's right sat Ellen Meloy, who was too shy, I reckoned, to say much. I'd have to think of some way to identify myself pretty quick, but what? I glanced up from the words I had been scribbling—"How about A.'s mother, Mildred, Mild-Ed"?—and back toward the door. At that moment a pink toy poodle pranced a few steps into the room trailing its leash, stopped, performed a triple take, sniffed the carpet, looked at me—paused—and reversed field back out the door.

That, at least, is the way I remember it.

Actually, my friend Marilyn had arranged for me to appear on five panels that day, back to back, without so much as a lunch break. ("Bring a sack. Chew with your mouth closed.") It may be that Sherman Alexie and Chief Mankiller were actually somewhere else. Maybe Terry Williams was actually one of the copanelists and Ellen Meloy and I were on one of the other panels together that day. I don't know for sure. But I could check.

The only thing I'm really sure about is that pink poodle.

And that pink poodle is for me the only inexplicably logical element in what I continue to think of as "typical Abbey doings," the extended weirdness of going on after Abbey.

When Ed came in 1984 to give the Stegner lecture at the college where I teach, he presented Tanya and me with a signed copy of the definitive, uncensored edition of *The Monkey Wrench Gang*, with R. Crumb's illustrations. He was headed for Missoula, Ed said, to give a watered-down version of the same lecture: "Free Speech: The Cowboy and His Cow." It was my first year as an assistant professor, and the college president and his wife had offered to host a dinner at their home in Ed's honor. According to my dean, the president had been the only one to vote against my appointment the previous spring. I thought about the invitation—such an opportunity for revenge—but declined politely without consulting anyone, mostly out of respect for Ed. As usual, Abbey packed the house for his lecture and insulted everyone personally, including the president's wife. In all, we spent three days together, two before and one after Ed's lecture. We took a series of brisk walks along the Snake and Clearwater rivers, haunted the mouth of Hell's Canyon, ate Tanya's homemade tortillas and enchiladas, and drank (in moderation) our way to television and radio interviews. I arranged for Ed to get a prescription for his pills from a physician friend of mind, and Abbey painfully passed a kidney stone the size of a tiny garnet without too much incident.

The crucial question came on the last day.

Ed and Tanya had gotten close on Ed's tramps from his motel to our ghetto apartment. Ed had approved of our marriage from the first—not that I needed his blessing—and together that week Tanya and Ed and I had discussed such mundane topics as illegal immigration, green chile, motherhood, Catholicism, mythology, Coors beer, Beethoven, Mozart, and mariachi music. On this morning, however, Ed and I drove to the levee before a scheduled breakfast and took a last hike. After we had stopped to watch a nearly naked girl on rollerblades sail by in the opposite direction, I could tell Ed had something to say.

I believe his precise words were, "Now what?"

I expressed surprise that they referred to me.

"Where are you going to live? What are you going to do?"

Words to that effect. "*How* are you going to live? Tanya isn't going to be very happy here, is she?"

"Jesus Christ, Ed," I said, "You can't be serious."

He shrugged. And grinned.

"This is my home," I said, "I belong here. I'm from Idaho. All of it. These are my people."

"You mean the Reverend Butler and the Aryan Nations? The Mormons? Or these other fools, the cowboys and the coygirls, the granola eaters, the schoolmarms?" He stopped to fish two cigars from his shirt pocket. I took one.

I don't know what else he said or what else I said. We each lighted and smoked part of the cigars. I think maybe our wives were both pregnant again that year. But although I've forgotten the words he used, I do know now just as I knew then exactly what he was saying. He talked a lot about doing work he had hated, the kind of work I'd done, too, but he talked even more about doing the work he loved. He was fifty-seven years old. He had written and published twenty books. He'd been married and divorced more times than I had. Certainly he'd traveled more widely and to much better purpose. Still, he had plenty of things he wanted to accomplish, but he was dying. I think he knew it and maybe he tried to let me know it, but all I heard was his persistent prodding, the same sort of exhorting that he had done when I first became his student in English 597ax. He was urging me to tell myself the truth about my family situation and to get on with my own opportunities.

And now I begin to remember some of his other words:

ED: Ever hear of Tom Wolfe? The real Thomas Wolfe?

ME: Yeah, sure. Why?

ED: Just wondered if you knew something about home that

he didn't? Besides, teaching is a shameful occupation, second-rate, maybe even third-rate. You're a better writer than that.... If you're any good at teaching or writing, they'll probably fire you.

ME: But I'm on the tenure track.

ED: They'll try to do it anyway.

Sure enough.

A year after Ed died (1989; b. 1923), Norman Maclean died (1990; b. 1902). Two years after Norman died, Wallace Stegner died (1993; b. 1909), and right after Wally died, Bill Stafford died (1993; b. 1914). People have begun to complain. Barry Lopez tells me the only time we see each other is at funerals. He's right. We see each other too often.

Until this moment, I have been unable to write anything I liked about Ed Abbey or his work, and like most people, I think, I'm pretty indifferent to even the best that has been written about those subjects. For one thing, I'm still not sure what is actually there to be said.

Why *did* that S.O.B. make such a difference?

According to the conclusions of our panel, he didn't. Under the pretense of playing "devil's advocate," our chairman, Russell Martin, proposed that Abbey hadn't written but one book that "mattered," one book that will last and endure.

You guessed it. *Desert Solitaire.*

In the basement where I write when the weather turns too bitter for me to compose outside, I have an exchange of letters, photocopies, between Martin and Abbey. In fact, I have a pile of spoor Ed left behind on that last visit as well as my own assorted collections of droppings: photographs, notebooks, notes, posters, newspaper clippings. When I reminded Ed that he'd left the notebook and photographs at our place, he suggested I dispose of them in the nearest trash can.

I stand as ready as anyone does to concede that not everything Edward Abbey wrote needs to see daylight. When I was a graduate student at the University of Arizona taking Abbey, Scott Momaday, and Richard Shelton, I was the first to make a futile attempt to catalog the boxes of debris Ed entrusted to our library's Special Collections. I found and read plenty of junk and catalogued by hand thousands of book reviews, letters, manuscripts, screenplays—the works —only to have Ed rearrange the materials I was attempting to process. (Over a beer after class, sometimes he would say something like, "Have you seen that film treatment I did of *Black Sun* anywhere?")

But I confess that I read his journals with some deliberation and care. In them I discovered a moveable feast, including fragments of poems Ed had copied verbatim from Robinson Jeffers, Wallace Stevens, and even Eleanor Wiley. Therefore, I was but mildly astonished to encounter a few of those same fragments in the bound galleys of *Earth Apples* that arrived in the mail here at the house last year. Hoping that Ed's poems had not yet gone to the printer, I called Clarke to report the problem. Too late, she said, the book was already in press. Finally, Abbey's editor Dave Petersen rode in like the Lone Ranger, stopped the presses, and corrected the errors. I doubt that it would have been the end of American literature if Dave hadn't corrected them and published the book.

Personally, I have never been able to find more than a couple of Ed's original poems that I thought even worthy of print, but I'm glad Dave published them. I'd probably have titled the book *Road Apples*. But *Earth Apples* is to *Desert Soli-*

taire what Eliot's cat poems are to *The Waste Land:* a footnote.
True: as an alleged scholar I'm supposed to deal in footnotes,
but that only brings me back to the question before us. So
let's look at the footnotes, at the record in Abbey's journal,
dated April 1983:

> My self-graded report card, à la Vonnegut:
>> *Jonathan Troy:* D–
>> *Brave Cowboy:* B
>> *Fire on the Mountain:* C
>> *Black Sun:* A
>> *Monkey Wrench Gang:* B
>> *Good News:* B
>> *Desert Solitaire:* B
>> *Abbey's Road:* A
>> *Journey Home:* C

If we calculate these grades using Abbey's own fifteen-point
scale (A+ = 15, F– = 1) we arrive at a total of 89 points out of
a possible 135 divided by the number of books listed (9) for
an average of 9.09 (C+, just short of a B–). Better than average, though, if you're judging yourself against the best that
women and men have thought and written for over two
thousand years. Of course, as a lefthanded, mule-stubborn
schoolmarm back in the early 1980s, Abbey unknowingly
punched a few sacred cows in the chest with this system
of his.

I'll never forget, for instance, the long line of graduate
students I encountered one day in the hall, a line leading directly to the office door of the director of creative writing. It
was Abbey's first semester at Arizona and her first semester
as director. Abbey had just handed back our first essays the
afternoon before. Instructors in the creative writing pro-

gram were supposed to award grades to graduate students only *after* they had completed the entire curriculum of their required writing classes and an MFA thesis. Not Ed. My paper read "B." I was impressed. So, I think, was Nancy Mairs with her grade, whatever it was. Too many others, however, were less sanguine, although plenty red-faced, and they were making it their business there in the director's office to see that such an error would never be repeated. Happily, it was, for those few who managed to tuck their tails between their legs and return to class. For my tuition money, a C from Abbey would have proved a good investment; an A for the course felt undeserved, but when I protested, Ed got silly: "Who's the teacher for this here course?"

"Physician," I said, "Heal thyself."

"Right," he grinned. "Like I said: A."

But for *Desert Solitaire*, allegedly his single masterpiece, he gave himself a B.

Go figure.

In *Collecting Abbey*, Spencer Maxwell puts the value of a first printing copy of *Desert Solitaire* (1968) between $250 and $450; *Jonathan Troy* (1954) between $1,500 and $2,500; *The Brave Cowboy* (1956) between $2,000 and $3,500; *Fire on the Mountain* (1962) between $600 and $1,200; *Black Sun* (1971) between $100 and $200; *The Monkey Wrench Gang* (1975) between $100 and $350; *The Journey Home* (1977) between $50 and $85; *Abbey's Road* (1979) between $175 and $300; *Good News* (1980) between $45 and $75; *Down the River* (1982) between $175 and $350 . . . all depending on the condition of the copy, of course. Who knows? If these ridiculous prices hold, the Hepworth children may eventually be able to attend college.

One of my undergraduate students in American literature

once asked, "Dr. Hepworth, what if Abbey had never written *Desert Solitaire?*"

Before I could reply, another student said, "But he did."

While it might be convenient to simply dismiss Abbey's other books from consideration to answer the very first question that Marilyn Auer posed for our panel that day— "Edward Abbey: Why Did That S.O.B. Make Such a Difference?"—to do so would be to ignore our stranglehold on the obvious, as well as a considerable amount of literary history, especially out here in the sticks, and not the least of that history concerns Abbey's novels. Not everything gold glitters, of course (although as Ed used to say, "All gold *is* fool's gold"). But let's get serious for a moment. What other American novel published in the 1970s has had as profound an effect on politics in the United States as *The Monkey Wrench Gang?*

Some days I wonder if anyone out there even remembers the 1970s. The Nixon-Ford-Carter years? Kent State (1969)? The first landing on the moon (1969)? James Dickey (*Deliverance*). Richard Brautigan (*Trout Fishing in America*). Ernest Gaines (*The Autobiography of Miss Jane Pittman*). Jerzy Kosinski (*Being There*). John Updike (*Rabbit Redux*). John Gardner (*Sunlight Dialogues, October Light*). Ishmael Reed (*Mumbo Jumbo*). Erica Jong (*Fear of Flying*). Saul Bellow (*Humboldt's Gift*). John Barth (*Letters*). E. L. Doctorow (*Ragtime*). Or some of Abbey's favorites: John Irving (*The World According to Garp*). Kurt Vonnegut (*Breakfast of Champions, Slapstick*). Thomas Pynchon (*Gravity's Rainbow*). All books published in the 1970s.

Assuredly, legions of Abbey's readers are simply too young to remember. So, hey. Who cares? Let's go blow up Glen Canyon Dam. Or how about this? We replant some grizzly bears in our national forests along with a few packs of timber

wolves. And while we're at it, maybe we could reestablish a
bison range out there in eastern Montana along the highline
clear into the Dakotas and through that long, sparsely populated strip of the Missouri River Breaks . . . Is it merely coincidence that Rachel Carson published *Silent Spring* in 1962,
Edward Abbey published *Desert Solitaire* in 1968, and that
one year later Congress passed the National Environmental
Policy Act?

These events do, in fact, coincide; they concur and accord
and even harmonize. I also believe what the FBI and other
agencies of the federal government only thought they might
learn when they first began to take an official interest in Edward Abbey on Lincoln's birthday back in 1947: this man will
do extreme things to achieve what he wants. (On that occasion he pinned to a bulletin board a note advocating the
burning of draft cards.) In a word, Edward Abbey is dangerous. Risky, unsafe. And that's why he made such a difference.
He knew, as George Washington (and after him, George
Washington Hayduke) put it, "Freedom, not safety, is the
highest good." And Abbey's life is a dramatization of that
principle.

His novels are one of the by-products of that life, and in
this sense they are at once both revolutionary and counter-
revolutionary: engines that help drive those cycles and gears
of momentous change necessary to maintain a free society
and assist our natural evolution toward becoming a truly civilized people, which means the books are also no more than
the wooden shoes of a saboteur, homemade mechanisms for
destroying the great machines responsible for our advanced
retrogression into the Dark Age in which we live. (Abbey:
"Civilization is a youth with a Molotov Cocktail in his
hand," the primitive Hayduke out to save "the fucking wilderness." Culture is "the L.A. cop who guns him down.")

In other words, Abbey's books are not meant to improve the world. (What a notion!) To Abbey, the world is sacred. It can't be improved. Lao-tzu: "If you tamper with it, you'll ruin it. Treat it like an object, you'll lose it."

Consider these lines from *The Monkey Wrench Gang*: "They had to build a whole new power plant to supply energy to the power plant which was the same power plant the power plant supplied—the wizardry of reclamation engineers!" Or these:

> Somebody had removed the Colorado River. . . . Instead of a river [Hayduke] looked down on a motionless body of murky green effluent, dead, stagnant, dull, a scum of oil floating on the surface. On the canyon walls a coating of dried silt and mineral salts, like a bathtub ring, recorded high-water mark. Lake Powell: storage pond, silt trap, evaporation tank and lagoon.

Perhaps the most serious charge against *The Monkey Wrench Gang* is that the novel promotes and glorifies violence. After all, it spawned much of the radical environmental movement: not just acts of civil disobedience but Earth First! Those tree-spiking Nazis with ambitions to blow up all dams on the Columbia at once. But if you live where I do, just a short two-hour drive from the real neo-Nazi headquarters at Hayden Lake, and only another hour from Sandpoint and Mark Fuhrman's new house, and less than two hours from "Almost Heaven," the Bo Gritz coven and paramilitary training ground for skinheads, Kluxer dropouts, and dildo-headed creeps of every nondescript description, you know, you really do, just from the reported news on the public radio and in the local tabloids, that the Earth First!ers are much more likely to put shit in the air-blown ventilators of some

Forest Service office or chain themselves to the handiest trunk of one of the last old-growth cedars than they are to even set off a string of firecrackers in a national forest. On the other hand, just listening to the same reports about the others or attending a militia meeting, you soon realize that individuals in these factions, perhaps even a majority of them, are not only fully capable of murder and rape but are actively looking for some provocation to serve their violent will upon "the people," namely the small town where you live, including your wife and three children, who just happen to be of Anglo-Saxon, Spanish, and Indian extraction. The next time you look a cop in the eye, one of our Idaho militiamen was quoted as saying, get a good look because the next time you might have to blow his face off.

Oh, well.

You're just an average guy, a WASP without a stinger, an "Anglo-Saxon Protestant Heterosexual Male," a kind of dinosaur, really, but one individual, nevertheless, who represents the last hope of the world, for as Abbey's friend Wendell Berry puts it, you have no excuses, nobody to blame but yourself. Who is going to sit at your feet and listen while you bewail your "historical sufferings"? White people in paradise. Who "will ever believe that we also have wept in the night with repressed longing to become our real selves? Who will stand forth and proclaim that we have virtues and talents peculiar to our category?"

Nobody.

And Mr. Berry sees that as good: for otherwise how could we rise up to meet, to actually create our "real selves in the real world"?

Ah, yes. Creation.

Maybe it is time to quiet our hearts and settle down for a

change, to remake the bed, to water the garden, to fold and sort the laundry, to go fishing or play music, and then perform "a few centuries of honest work."

Those few who have dared to closely read *The Monkey Wrench Gang* (I can never remember if it has sold only half a million or a million copies) will have to conclude that, like Abbey's other books, one of its strengths is that it offers us no "quick-fix" solutions. They will also have to conclude, as Ann Ronald does in her reading, that even the most openly "violent" member of the fictional Monkey Wrench Gang is pretty tame. He may be a veteran of jungle warfare, but he is also a "Lone Ranger of comically pseudomythic proportions."

Here are the words of Abbey's narrator (not Abbey, as Ronald mistakenly writes): "George Hayduke had never killed a man. Not even a Vietnamese man. Not even a Vietnamese woman. Not even a Vietnamese child." Doc Sarvis, admittedly the character closest to Abbey's own persona, insists: "We are law-abiding people." But finally, consider this:

> "What's more American than violence?" Hayduke wanted to know. "Violence, it's as American as pizza pie."
> "Chop suey," said Bonnie.
> "Chile con carne."
> "Bagels and lox."

In *The Monkey Wrench Gang*, nobody dies. Nobody even gets hurt. Which may be why Hollywood has so frequently taken out options and never gotten around, somehow, to actually making a film. (We have only to imagine other reasons: the destruction of property in the defense of the earth might set off the ticking bombs already in the hands of the masses.) The real problem set forth playfully in *The Monkey Wrench Gang*, as Abbey himself knew intimately, is that the improper

violent destruction of the physical engines of our deep retrogression—the hydroelectric dams, the atomic generators
and missiles, the oil wells of Iraq and Kuwait and New Mexico—will produce only its own series of ecological disasters.
The book does not devalue this truth.

The true problem is knowledge, and the only solution,
love. We are terrifyingly ignorant. For one thing, like Adam
and Eve, we know too much, and one of the things we know
is that the acquisition of knowledge is merely the revelation
of ignorance. Here again, of course, I'm paraphrasing Mr.
Berry: "Our problems tend to gather under two questions
about knowledge: Having the ability and desire to know,
how and what should we learn? And, having learned, how
and for what should we use what we know?" We should be
ever mindful, Berry insists, that people with far less information than we have have found better solutions. Give two
farmers the same tools, techniques, and information, and one
will ruin land while both might just as easily have saved and
improved it.

Is Mr. Berry, then, a champion of ignorance? Was Abbey?

No. But both men demand that we put knowledge in its
place, that we abandon our superstitious beliefs: that knowledge is "ever sufficient," that it can *itself* solve problems; that
it is "intrinsically good," that "it can be used objectively or
disinterestedly." A "disinterested" or "objective" researcher
is a contradiction in terms, merely a euphemism for someone
who works for the "side that pays best."

Where, then, is our hope and our salvation?

For answers, let's turn now to the most critical statement,
the most succinct, and arguably the most representative of
our spirit as a nation and a people over the course of the last
four centuries: "The destiny of man is to possess the whole
earth; the destiny of the earth is to be subject to man. There

can be no full conquest of the earth and no real satisfaction
to humanity, if large portions of the earth remain beyond his
highest control." Written by a Mormon patriarch at the
height of the irrigation campaigns, it is a tenet that outrages
me to the very depths of my Jack Mormon soul. Compare
that statement with these:

> All things were made by him; and without him was not any-
> thing made that was made. (John 1:3)

> The earth is the Lord's, and the fulness thereof: the world and
> they that dwell therein. (Psalms 24:1)

> The land is mine; for ye are strangers and sojourners with
> me. (Leviticus 25:23)

Abbey's life and his work command us to "love the earth,"
which is one way of commanding us to love God, if you understand, as I do, God to mean Creation and, further, the
presence of deity, not apart from Creation, but within it.
Everywhere in his life and his work Abbey also urges us to
find ways to live in the places we have chosen without killing
them, and he makes it abundantly clear that there can never
be any replication of the earth. Our destruction of Creation
is more than putrid economics, irresponsible stewardship,
and treachery to our family obligations. It is, in Berry's
words, "the most horrid blasphemy, the flinging of God's
gifts into his face, as if they were of no worth beyond that
assigned to them by our destruction of them." William Kit-
tredge puts it this way: "There will never be another setup
like the one in which we have thrived." Abbey himself writes:

> The love of wilderness is more than a hunger for what is al-
> ways beyond reach; it is also an expression of loyalty to the
> earth, the earth which bore us and sustains us, the only home

we shall ever know, the only paradise we ever need—if only
we had the eyes to see. Original sin, the true original sin, is
the blind destruction for the sake of greed of this natural paradise which lies all around us—if only we were worthy of it.

All of which brings me back to that pink poodle who strayed
into the discussion at the outset of this essay. It reminded me
of everything French, from King Louis XVI and poor Marie-
Antoinette to the storming of the Bastille and the guillotine,
Rousseau, Molière, Montaigne, Céline, Sartre, Camus . . .
and not least of the words of that part-time Parisian from
Monticello who wrote that "whenever any form of government becomes destructive of these ends [life, liberty, and the
pursuit of happiness], it is the right of the people to alter or
to abolish it, and to institute new government, laying its
foundation on such principles, and organizing its powers in
such form, as to them shall seem most likely to effect their
safety and happiness."

For me, that poodle was like an Abbey sighting. It would
be typical of his incongruous character to bait us with the
promise that he would return to life in his next incarnation
as a vulture and then show up as a poodle. For me, that
Frenchified token of fur is a reminder that in our government revolutions happen with almost dizzying regularity,
like a spinning wheel threatening to speed out of control.
From our beginnings as a nation, change has in fact been the
only constant in American life, especially for our most invisi-
ble minority, Native Americans, whose tenure on the North
American continent, as we all know, predates the European
voyages of exploration and so-called discovery by tens of mil-
lennia.

One result is that now all sorts of people—the loggers and
millworkers of Idaho and Oregon, fishermen from Maine to

Washington, ranchers, farmers, women in general—currently find themselves and their families in the position of John Vogelin in Abbey's third novel, *Fire on the Mountain*. They are about to be forcibly removed and displaced. It is essentially the same position our first people knew personally and privately each day as dawn rose over the graves of their parents and grandparents. In the overwhelming majority of cases, along with the genetic variety of their plants and animals, we exterminated even their languages, so that they might not speak the violence of their truth against us, or if they still sought to do so, they could speak it only in the broken tongue of their faithless conquerors. We made contract after contract with that America. In our world now remote from theirs in time, we little note nor long remember what we said in those covenants, but we have never forgotten what we did with them: we cracked, split, and shattered them.

Edward Abbey knew that each day of our lives we are engaged, if we choose to be, in a great civil war of love, testing whether our nation, or any nation conceived in liberty and dedicated to the proposition that all men are created equal, can long endure. He knew that it is for us, the living, to dedicate ourselves to the unfinished work of those cherished men and women who fought and died to advance our cause so nobly. He was not the Abe Lincoln of our literature. He was Edward Abbey, a great patriot. In all of our literature there is no one quite like him. As he did in life, he stands alone, as unique as Walt Whitman.

But Abbey was also what one of his teachers, Wallace Stegner, called him, "a red-hot moment in the conscience of our country." And unlike too many of us, Edward Abbey lived up to Plato's expectation for every free citizen "to know thy self."

Small wonder, then, that when a "lit cricket" named Russell Martin referred in print to Abbey as a "smirking pessi-
mist," Abbey characteristically responded to the critic with
criticism, for Edward Abbey not only submitted himself and
his work to criticism but, like Norman Maclean, he virtually
demanded it. Predictably, young Mr. Martin leaped into the
defensive trench where he soon began to thump very loudly
upon his lexicon:

> You don't like "smirking pessimist." Well, smirking, in my
> dictionary, means "smiling in a knowing or annoyingly com-
> placent way." Your work is full of a strong, ironic, pessimistic
> voice that seems certain that the wild country will be de-
> stroyed. Yet you rightly see a kind of black comedy in that, a
> joy in chaos, as I said. Smirking pessimist seems right to the
> point to me. . . . I'm amazed that you seem so thin-skinned
> about this sort of thing.

A month later came Abbey's second reply:

> I resent . . . being called a pessimist, smirking or not, because
> it is false. I am not a pessimist. And to say that I have written
> off, given up on, the West is a lie. A damnable lie. If it were
> true I would no longer spend half of my time trying to help
> save what's left of the West. The ones who have given up are
> those who complain that environmentalists "depress" them,
> who claim they care about the West but are too fastidious to
> get down off the fence and help fight for it. In my eyes, such
> half-assed "Westerners" are no better than common tour-
> ists, whether they've resided out here for ten years or fifty.

Martin found Abbey's novel *Good News* "tedious" and "de-
pressing," which in my mind's dictionary connotes drudgery
and labor—in other words, real work. In fact, the proper
reading of a novel *is* work, and arguably among the most dif-

ficult kinds of work, requiring some knowledge of history, strict self-discipline, hours of concentration and mental strain. So who needs it? Isn't the author's job, in the words of Sir Philip Sidney, to "teach and delight," in short, to entertain? Is Bach entertaining or just tedious? Or how about Mahler? Beethoven? Mozart? Why read those crumbling sandblocks of literature like Joyce's *Ulysses* and *Finnegans Wake*, Pynchon's *Gravity's Rainbow*, all that stuff by Dostoyevsky, Kafka, Melville, Faulkner, Homer, Milton, Dante . . . ? Why read books so dense and obtuse they tax the understanding of our greatest readers, who are, of course, chiefly other writers: Pound, Stein, Malcolm X, Gandhi . . . ?

Now that another revolution has occurred, it has become fashionable to say that the salmon are gone along with the buffalo, to whine and complain that we've run out of room, that our society is no match for the remnants of our scenery, and above all, that we need new stories to live by.

Instead of complaining, we might try writing some. Who knows, I may even try myself. That's what Ed Abbey did. His work is now our work, and as always it is unfinished and a long series of labors ready to be taken up lies before us, including the proper reading of his novels. And if we are to survive and create the revolutionary free society he imagined, we must indeed commit ourselves to such violences as he did. In short, we must act, for violence primarily means action, the exertion of physical force. But we must also be as clear and deliberate in our violence as he was, which means we must act properly and responsibly in regard to all life, human and inhuman.

Edward Abbey's words have obviously outlived him. What more could a writer hope for?

Plenty, I think, but above all, that his words will inspire both the smallest and greatest deeds of those who come after, for no proper action is too humble to make a difference in our insane world, and we all know that too many great and brave deeds must go unacknowledged. Is there a prescription for violences, then, that might heal or remit our madness? Yes, but all issues are particulars, and the remedy so specific for each one that we will be unable to reach for it from that open door of acclaim, censure, and rules. Tree planting might suffice. So might organic gardening. Better yet, organic farming. Voting. Writing letters to politicians. Stuffing envelopes. Suffering fools in committee hearings. Paying tithes to environmental organizations and public radio. Composing music. Boycotting certain products. Phone calling. Protesting ignorance and injustice. I suppose that day may even come when human monsters stand ready to break down our doors, in which case conscience and duty will require us to take extreme action that will endanger lives. Regardless, the telling of truth in whatever form always constitutes a considerable violence and risk, a movement of momentous force against the seemingly more powerful counterfeit forces of falsity, prevarication, sham, fraud, forgery, quackery, imitation, and all manner of deception and lies.

For his part, Ed Abbey told the truth, mainly. In his own words, "he done his best."

Did his life and his work make a difference?

You bet.

DAVE SOLHEIM AND ROB LEVIN

The *Bloomsbury Review*
Interview

Dave Solheim and Rob Levin conducted the following composite interview with Edward Abbey. It first appeared in the November/December 1980 issue of *The Bloomsbury Review*, a bold, bimonthly magazine devoted to writers and books on the American West. At the time of the interview, Dave Solheim was a graduate student in creative writing at the University of Denver, Rob Levin a reporter for *The Arizona Daily Star*. Solheim and Levin prefaced their interview with the two paragraphs below:

"Probably more than any other living writer, Edward Abbey is the spokesman for the American West. He has published six novels (the most recent of which, *Good News*, is reviewed in this issue) and eight books of non-fiction essays and travelogues. Although he is one of the leading spokesmen for the preservation of wilderness, he defies labels. He believes in wilderness first of all for its own sake, and secondly because it allows human beings to have feelings of danger and freedom which are too often removed from modern life. He is not the new Thoreau of anything, but will wear, if somewhat uncomfortably, the labels of anarchist and wild preservationist. But don't let that fool you. Abbey is as diverse and slippery as the slickrock country he writes about and as predictable as a flashflood.

"Abbey lives at home in the desert southwest near Tucson with his wife and two dogs, Bones and Elly. The dogs are like him in that they prefer to spend the day wandering the desert. His clothing frequently looks government issued, maybe left over from his previous work as a park ranger, forest ranger, and fire lookout. He wears combat boots made in Taiwan. 'They feel good; they wear well.' Though he may at first appear as a slightly disheveled Smokey the Bear, Abbey is far from G.I. He is consistently radical, but relishes the complications and contradictions of being human."

––––––––

THE BLOOMSBURY REVIEW: In some of your novels, major characters seem to be killed only to return to life later: Jack Burns in *The Brave Cowboy* and in *Good News*, and George Hayduke in *The Monkey Wrench Gang*. Are you too attached to your characters to finally kill them off, or is there more justification for these resurrections than I have noticed?

EDWARD ABBEY: I believe in happy endings, and furthermore, I do not understand my own books, very well, anyway. Jack Burns also appears in *The Monkey Wrench Gang*. I do like to keep my endings open. The first edition of *The Brave Cowboy* was too closed, but I corrected that in the later editions.

BLOOMSBURY: Can your readers expect to hear more of Hayduke or Burns in future novels?

ABBEY: Very likely.

BLOOMSBURY: Maybe the middle of Jack Burns's life?

ABBEY: That's a good idea.

BLOOMSBURY: George Hayduke seems to be a sociopath. He wants to drive his jeep and throw his empty beer cans wherever he wants to. Is even the West big enough for more than one or two Haydukes? Do you have any reservations about presenting such a character in a favorable light?

ABBEY: Hayduke is Hayduke. I do not feel responsible for his behavior.

BLOOMSBURY: *The Monkey Wrench Gang* suggests that old four-wheel drives are good and that new ones deserve to have boulders dropped on them; that it's OK to use a chain saw on billboards, but not on trees. Is that important to the novel?

ABBEY: I think that I shall never see a billboard lovely as a tree.

BLOOMSBURY: At the end of *Desert Solitaire* you suggest that both the city and the wilderness are necessary for modern human existence. *Good News*, your latest novel, opens presenting "the oldest civil war, that between the city and the country." Does this show a change in your thinking or did your idea of balance include the tension of conflict or even war?

ABBEY: All of the above. I'd like to live fairly near a city, but I don't have any desire to live in a city. Where I'm at now suits me fine. If it'd stay this way, I could live here the rest of my life. But very likely, this will all be built up in a few years.

I'd like to live fifty or sixty miles out in the country from a city like Tucson or Santa Fe. Or Salt Lake. Or five hundred miles out in the country and get an airplane and a pilot's license.

As I've said before, I'm not a recluse or a hermit. I like some social life. I'd like to have the best of both worlds. The wilderness and urban civilization.

BLOOMSBURY: You are noted for the political-activist stance of your novels. Do you have to control your characters to serve your political ends?

ABBEY: I try to control my characters, but they almost always get out of hand. They like to go their own ways.

BLOOMSBURY: I have a half-baked theory that one distinguishing feature of western literature is that the landscape is an active character, a participant in the events of a novel; that the landscape acts on, and interacts with, the human characters. In *Good News* landscape is replaced by a burned-out cityscape. Is that important?

ABBEY: I certainly agree that the landscape is a major character in most western novels, and probably should be. But I also believe that the land acts upon and shapes human beings everywhere, eastern as well as western, city as well as country.

BLOOMSBURY: I guess that takes care of my theory.

ABBEY: I do think that you're right. The land, the earth of the American West, is unique. It acts in ways that are hard to describe.

BLOOMSBURY: In your introduction to *Abbey's Road*, you mention a number of writers whom you respect. You seem to be the only western writer I'm familiar with (except for Tom Robbins, whom you don't mention and might not be a western writer) who has an urbane, ironic wit in your work. Would you comment on that, or correct me where I'm wrong?

ABBEY: Well, I'm not a Tom Robbins fan. I like his first book, *Another Roadside Attraction*. I tried to read *Even Cowgirls Get the Blues* but could not get through it. It's just too cutesy-pie for me. I regard him as a kind of shampoo artist or a cotton-candy vendor. Writers whom I really admire who live in, or write about the West are: William Eastlake, Wallace Stegner, Tom McGuane, Wright Morris, Larry McMurtry, and I think all of them have plenty of wit and irony.

BLOOMSBURY: Would you discuss a few of your favorite writers, both classic and contemporary, and tell why they are your favorites?

ABBEY: Well, I suppose it's much more interesting, isn't it, opinions on contemporary writers. We all admire Shakespeare and Tolstoy, or most of us do. There's nothing much new to say about them. Well, I like McGuane and Pynchon. Oh, Christ, I'm not much of a critic, I'm not very good at analyzing things. I think it's probably a matter of style. I just admire very much the way they write, the way they handle the language. Have you read Pynchon? *Gravity's Rainbow?* It's almost incomprehensible to me. I find great difficulty in what the hell he's saying as I go along, but I read it anyway. I enjoy it. I find it fascinating, even though it's so complex and dense and obscure and mysterious that I don't know quite what he's saying.

McGuane is a very clear writer, although he has opaque paragraphs here and there. His writing always has a kind of bloodchilling nihilism to it that I can't always find appealing. But it's interesting, it's powerful.

Another contemporary writer I admire would be William Eastlake, also a friend of mine. He lives down in Bisbee, a small town about ninety miles southeast of Tucson, on the border. He wrote some novels about life in New Mexico. He wasn't very serious about it. He wrote three novels about contemporary New Mexico. And they are marvelous novels. Indians and cowboys and jazz musicians and tourists and ranchers and written in a very witty, ironic style. Eastlake is also a master of the sentence and paragraph.

And there's Alan Harrington. I might as well put in another plug for a writer and friend who lives out here in Tucson. He, I think, is a great essayist. He wrote the book *The Immortalist. The Immortalist* is not a novel. It's a 300-page essay on the subject of death and immortality—the very things we were told to avoid as journalism students. It's a very interesting book, full of interesting ideas. And Alan has also written some good novels, mostly about New York life. He was a New Yorker for about twenty years. He moved out here about ten years ago. And he just finished a novel a few days ago called *The White Rainbow*, which is about Mexico and the old Aztec traditions, human sacrifice—kind of a morbid book, but very interesting. I've read parts of it and he's read parts of it to me.

I like Nabokov quite a lot. I was shocked that he did not get the Nobel Prize. I admire him chiefly as a stylist, a master of the language. He's a Russian who can write English much better than many of us Americans.

B. Traven is another literary hero of mine. He's not such a well-known American writer, if he was American. His whole life was sort of a mystery. He may have been born in Germany. He lived most of his life in Mexico. He wrote *The Treasure of Sierra Madre*, which became the famous movie. But he wrote about half a dozen other novels which are just as good. His best was one called *The Death Ship*, about a sailor's life in the merchant marines in the 1920s.

Well, I could go on and on. There are many living writers I admire. I think there's a helluva lot of challenge here in the United States. No writer that I would call great. I don't think we have another Faulkner among us. But who knows. Pynchon is still fairly young, and so is McGuane. I think they're both in their thirties.

BLOOMSBURY: At least for the last few years you have lived in the rural Southwest. How important is that location for your writing? Would you be as significant a writer as you are now if you had continued to live in New Jersey or New York?

ABBEY: That's a good way to phrase it. I sometimes suspect I might have been a better writer if I'd stayed back East; it's a lot easier to sit indoors there. But I don't think I'd be so happy a man. The Southwest is definitely my home, and I think it always will be. At least I hope so. I've lived here a long time. Since 1947 except for a year in Europe and one year in New York. So I've lived most of my life in the Southwest.

BLOOMSBURY: Is there one state or town that you consider home? You've said that you were going to leave here when your wife finished college. You've lived many other places. Does it make any difference so long as it's in the Southwest?

ABBEY: I call a very large area home. Parts of Mexico, Baja California, all the way up into parts of Wyoming. I don't think it matters very much. I really do regard the whole Southwest as my home. I'm perfectly happy to live anywhere in Arizona, New Mexico, Utah, Nevada. I like the desert; I like the hot, dry climate. I hate to be cold and wet, especially both at the same time.

BLOOMSBURY: You have said some harsh things about the New York publishing establishment. Your books have been published by large houses and reissued by the University of New Mexico Press. What role do you see that university presses, small presses, and non-commercial presses have in the world of publishing conglomerates?

ABBEY: I'm all for them. I think there will always be a role for the small presses and the university presses. They serve as outlets for scholarly work and for new and experimental fiction, and writing by new and unknown authors that the national publishers will not take a chance on. I think both of these presses are useful and necessary and always have been in American literature. You may recall that Thoreau paid for publication of his first book of which he sold two hundred copies out of a printing of two thousand. The advantage of big publishers is the large audience. A writer wants to be read by as many people as possible.

BLOOMSBURY: At this stage of your career, you probably have no need for it, but did you ever want to work in a community of writers? What do you think about university writing programs?

ABBEY: First of all, I don't have a career, only a life. Writing books is a passion. But it's only one of several passions. No, I would not want to work in a community of writers. Trying to live with one writer—myself—is difficult enough. Many other writers have influenced me, certainly. But they're not to blame for anything. As for college writing programs, I doubt if they do any harm.

If a student is interested in writing, or wants to become a writer, he probably should take a writing class. I took one or two when I was a student. They might teach you something, but most of all they give you pressure to write. That's the hardest thing about writing—to get started, to put the first things down on a page.

BLOOMSBURY: What makes you write now? When you've been loafing, hiking, hanging out for a year or so do you make notes on things? When do you decide you can't put it off any longer? Does the pressure to write keep building?

ABBEY: I do make notes. I have such a bad memory that I have to, or I'd forget everything.

There are two forms of pressure. One is psychological and the other is financial. I make my living by writing—mostly. I've also made a partial living from being a fire lookout.

You know, the psychological pressure builds up. If I'm not writing, I begin to feel guilty, useless. Sloth and bloat set in. I get itchy. I'm too much of a Puritan to be a good loafer, I guess. And also, I take assignments, do magazine articles, have to meet deadlines. . . .

BLOOMSBURY: In *Abbey's Road* you claim to wear a tie when you write. You aren't wearing one now.

ABBEY: I have worn a tie. I will probably die in one.

BLOOMSBURY: Several of your characters have spent time in jail. Have you?

ABBEY: Yes, I have been in jail a few times. Once for vagrancy, once for public drunkenness, once for reckless driving—what the police called "negligent driving"—rather trivial offenses. I'm not very proud of them. But I think it's important for a writer to spend at least one night in jail, maybe even more important for lawyers and judges. I have *not* been in jail for refusing to pay taxes. I tried to not pay taxes in the late sixties, but they just went to my employer at the time and garnished my wages.

BLOOMSBURY: Violence is in most of your writing. Has violence directly affected you in any way?

ABBEY: As for violence, I'm against it for I am a practical coward. However, violence is an integral part of the modern world, modern civilization, and I assume that someday I may have to face it. So I load my own ammo. There are a few things worth killing for. Not many, but a few.

BLOOMSBURY: Your master's thesis in philosophy was a study of the ethics of violence. I understand you were frustrated by restraints placed on it by the faculty committee?

ABBEY: Yes, I wanted to write a book that I was going to call the "General Theory of Anarchism." Fortunately, the thesis committee was not interested in that kind of tome, or I'd still be working on that first treatise.

BLOOMSBURY: Although you've been reluctant to talk about it, when you were the editor of *The Thunderbird*, the student literary magazine at the University of New Mexico, the university president suspended its publication for a year.

ABBEY: Well, in my case it was kind of a showoff stunt. It was sort of silly, but what I did was put a quote on the cover of this magazine that said: "Mankind will never be free until the last king is strangled by the entrails of the last priest." And I attributed that to Louisa May Alcott. False, of course. It was some Frenchman. Diderot, I believe. And of course, I got the Catholics in an uproar about that. I don't blame them. It was kind of a stupid thing to do. I was just trying to attract attention.

BLOOMSBURY: You said you were a practical coward?

ABBEY: Well, I try to avoid direct physical violence if possible. I've never been in a barroom fight. I've been in plenty of barrooms. Some close calls, but usually, always, I've been able to talk my way out of it. I haven't been in a fight since about the fourth grade when I beat up my best friend, the only guy in the class I could lick.

BLOOMSBURY: How do you feel about your work being the subject of academic study? Would you prefer a barroom discussion of your books to a classroom discussion?

ABBEY: I don't care where my books are read or by whom. I'm happy to be read by anybody, anywhere. I've no objection to people talking about them in a classroom or a barroom, as long as it's done voluntarily by willing victims.

BLOOMSBURY: They could be required reading.

ABBEY: Well, no one is required to go to college. At least not yet.

BLOOMSBURY: You aren't worried about what academic people might do to your work?

ABBEY: No. I don't think about it. Let them do their work. I'll do mine.

BLOOMSBURY: After people read your books, how would you like them to think of you, or do you care?

ABBEY: All writers need love, appreciation. I think I write mainly to please myself, because that's the easiest way for me to write. I don't have any analytical or critical ability. I cannot design a book very well. I write rapidly, spontaneously, out of the belly and bowels. And usually from a very personal point of view.

Most of my work doesn't get very good reviews, especially back East. I've got this grudge against New York book reviewers. I don't think they take me seriously. All western writers feel this way, though. All of us who live out here and write out here.

As I said, we all want to be loved, appreciated. Fame. The desire for fame is certainly one of the motives for writing. I suppose there's a danger in too much fame, too much money. I guess that could spoil a writer. I haven't had an opportunity to deal with that yet. But I'm willing to take the chance.

I think all writers are egotists. I wasn't much good at athletics. I couldn't even make the high school basketball team. Oh, I suppose it's true that artistic ability in writing is compensation for failure in some other line. But I wouldn't make much of that.

I think writers have it pretty good. Especially anybody that can make a living by writing, which I've been able to do for the last ten years. I'm a pretty lucky person, which doesn't necessarily mean I'll be happy.

BLOOMSBURY: You present yourself and seem to think of yourself as a novelist. Suppose, for the sake of argument, that you are considered to be more important as an essayist, or worse yet, a nature writer. How would that affect you and your writing?

ABBEY: I go my own way, do the best I can, writing mainly to please myself. But it is on the assumption that there is an audience out there somewhere, made up of people pretty much like myself, or at least of people who think and feel like me. So far that approach seems to work. I don't know whether I'm primarily a novelist or essayist or something in between. I don't really worry about that.

BLOOMSBURY: What would you say are your strengths and weaknesses as a writer?

ABBEY: I guess I'd have to divide fiction from non-fiction to answer that question. As an essayist—I like to call myself an essayist, it sounds good, instead of a journalist. I've said some nasty things about journalism, journalists. But I'm a journalist myself half the time, when I do my magazine writing. I was once editor of a small-town weekly. For six months I was editor of the Taos weekly newspaper. It went out of business, and I lost my job. I took journalism in high school, flunked it twice. Same course, flunked it twice. I just couldn't get the facts straight. I had a hard time making the news fit the page, doing the layouts. So all those nasty remarks I made about journalists were meant to be, hopefully, a put-on. But I would like to call myself an essayist. But anyway, getting on to the weaknesses. . . .

On non-fiction, and I've been criticized for this, I tend to be self-indulgent. I ramble on and on. I write too much about myself. Sometimes it works pretty well, but it can be over-done. After a while, the reader gets really tired of hearing about the writer's personal problems and opinions. He'd like a more objective point of view, a description of what's going on out there.

In fiction, I've published six novels now, and I wrote a couple of more that were unpublished, rejected. And I've got two or three more in my head that I want to write. My main difficulty in fiction, especially in novel form, is plotting. How to arrange the material in the most effective way. I just don't understand how you construct a plot. I generally follow the obvious, most simple way. Beginning at the beginning, follow a linear chronology. I tried writing short stories long, long ago. I found them even more difficult. There you really have to exercise discipline, know what you're doing. I'm not any good at that. For me, the novel is easier to write than the short story. You can get away with more looseness and carelessness. I can't say any more. I don't like to talk about my weaknesses.

BLOOMSBURY: You already have. But what about your strengths?

ABBEY: Oh, hell, I can't analyze my own work. I really just write to suit myself. I work very fast, in spasms and in spurts and loaf a lot between projects, books or articles. I think I write fast, but carelessly, but always pretty damn spontaneously, which may be both a strength and a weakness.

BLOOMSBURY: I've heard that you are working on an autobiographical novel. If that is so, it is from any attempt to merge the fiction and non-fiction writing you have done?

ABBEY: No. I've got some stories left and I want to write about one good, fat book and then perhaps I'll resign from my author business and do something different. I want to build a house. A stone house. Maybe an adobe houseboat. Raise my children, blow up something. I don't know.

BLOOMSBURY: Your novels might be seen to suggest that all attempts to make a living in the West are destructive. Are there ways to live here that don't destroy the land or humanity of the people?

ABBEY: I believe that farming, ranching, mining, logging are all legitimate, honorable, useful, and necessary enterprises. I respect and admire those who carry on these occupations. Especially those who do it in a way that treats the earth with love, and the rights of our posterity with respect. The problem, where things go wrong, is in scale, size, number. The carnage that we're doing to the American West, the planet as a whole, results, I think, mainly from too many people demanding more from the land than the land can sustain.

BLOOMSBURY: In *Good News* a minor character, Glenn, is a piano player who attempts to return to being a composer, a musician, even though he has no audience. Could he be seen as a metaphor for the role of the artist in the West?

ABBEY: No. I don't think so. That character is just being true to his way of life. He will go on making music even for an audience of one—himself. I don't think he's a metaphor for anything more.

BLOOMSBURY: Another character, Sam Banyaca, is a Zuni who presents himself as a magician, able only to do sleight of hand, yet at several key points in the novel, he performs with the real power of a shaman. Are you presenting Indian traditions of mystic power as viable for non-Indians in the modern, technological world?

ABBEY: I'd rather not explain that. There is an explanation for it in the novel that is bigger than you suggest, but I don't want to try to explain it. Yes, I do think Indian beliefs, traditions, and customs have much to teach us. We have much to learn.

BLOOMSBURY: Is there a difference between Sam and, say, Carlos Castaneda?

ABBEY: I've said all I want to say about Castaneda. Sam is a trickster and occupies a special position. There is a narrow line between magic tricks and power. A difference that won't quite fit in words.

BLOOMSBURY: Do you consider yourself a practical man or a romantic man?

ABBEY: I'm a practical romantic. I worry about making a living, raising my three children, getting my wife through college, paying my bills. I've got myself trapped in the same sort of mortgage situation as most other people around. But I have to make a living one way or the other. To that extent I'm a practical man.

BLOOMSBURY: To what extent are you a romantic?

ABBEY: Well, I love to be in love . . . with many things. I tell you, these are rather probing questions you're getting at here.

That's an interesting question, though. I do consider myself a romantic. Partially, I suppose, because I'm an idealist. I still think it's possible to find some better way to live, both as an individual and as a society.

And I have the usual romantic ills—thinking things must be more beautiful beyond the next range of hills. I've been fascinated by the mysterious and unknown. Those are romantic traits.

BLOOMSBURY: What is the worst possible future you see for the American West?

ABBEY: The worst possible future for the American West is already here. At least I hope it is the worst. I am an optimist. I believe that the industrial, military state will eventually collapse or destroy itself.

The horned toads, the hawks, and the coyotes and the rattlesnakes and other innocent creatures I hope will survive and carry on, and yes, probably a few humans with them, or at least I hope so. I think the human race will get one more chance. I'm not sure we deserve it, but I hope we get it anyway.

I look forward to the day when gasoline becomes so expensive and motor vehicles become so expensive that we all have to go back to horses and walking. I'm willing to give up my truck . . . if everybody else does. All right. Enough of that. You want to go for a walk?

Down the River with Edward Abbey

Tucson · May, 1984

Dear Ed,

The notion of writing *about* somebody I know and like makes me feel gossipy, and a little silly. So I'm writing *to* you and if anybody else wants to look over my shoulder while I do, that's all right with me. Even you can—if you want.

Just before beginning this piece, I reviewed the last, posthumously published book of a writer I often admire, the Argentine Julio Cortázar. The book is called *A Certain Lucas*, and in it there's this passage, which left me puzzled:

> A landscape, a stroll through the woods, a dousing in a waterfall, a road between two cliffs, can only raise up to aesthetic heights if we have the assurance of a return home or to the hotel, the lustral shower, dinner and wine, the talk over coffee and dessert, a book or some papers, the eroticism that sums everything up and starts it up again. I don't trust admirers of nature who every so often get out of the car to look at the view and take five or six leaps out onto the rocks; as for the others, those lifetime Boy Scouts who are accustomed to wandering about covered by enormous knapsacks and wild beards, their reactions are mostly monosyllabic or exclama-

tory; everything seems to consist of standing time and time again looking at a hill or a sunset, which are the most recurrent things imaginable.

Civilized people are lying when they fall into bucolic rapture; if they miss their Scotch on the rocks at seven thirty in the evening, they'll curse the minute they left home to come and endure gnats, sunburn, and thorns; as for those closest to nature, they're as stupid as it is. A book, a play, a sonata, don't need any return or shower; that's where we reach the greatest heights, where we are the most we can be. What the intellectual or the artist who takes refuge in the countryside is looking for is tranquility, fresh lettuce, and oxygenated air; with nature surrounding him on all sides, he reads or paints in the perfect light of a well-oriented room; if he goes out for a walk or goes to the window to look at the animals or the clouds, it's because he's tired with his work or with his ease. Don't trust, then, the absorbed contemplation of a tulip when the contemplator is an intellectual. What's there is tulip + distraction or tulip + meditation (almost never about the tulip). You will never find a natural scene that can take more than five minutes of determined contemplation, and, on the other hand, you will feel all time abolished in the reading of Theocritus or Keats, especially in the passages where scenes of nature appear.

Perhaps I shouldn't have been puzzled. Cortázar spent most of the last half of his life in Paris, a place that has addled more brains than his. But he wasn't a fool; I'd read enough of his work to know that. And after all, he was an Argentine, a native of a country that has more wildness left in it than even this one does. It couldn't be that he'd never had a chance to see anything beyond Rimbaud's "cold puddle of Europe." Even given the Argentine's most fervent wish to out-Europe Europe in urbanity and "civilization," surely he had read Thoreau, at least—if not Edward Abbey. And where did he think Keats and Theocritus came up with those "passages where scenes of nature appear" in the first place? What was wrong with the man that he could say such patently idiotic things? Or was he saying something I was missing (he did that from time to time)?

Then I reread *Down the River*, and I realized that he was saying something *he* was missing. I'll explain. In a round-about way.

In one sense or another, all the essays and articles in *Down the River* are about things of the earth, with a couple of other topics thrown in for the sake of inconsistency (we're on to you, Abbey). Not everything in it was written for inclusion between the covers of a single book: it's a collection of pieces you wrote over several years for a number of publications and reasons. Nonetheless, they're all surges, eddies, waves, rocks in the same stream, all ways of reaching for *la motif*, as your friend Debris calls it in one of the book's essays. And as you say in your introduction, together they have a common purpose (like Cortázar's books, sonatas, and plays, I imagine), "to serve as antidotes to despair."

There's another function the essays serve, too. Like all of your work, like any serious writer's work, they serve to define who you are as a writer and, if John Gardner was right in saying that we are our best selves when we are writing, who you are as a man. If that's presumption, so be it. Gardner was right.

Take the first essay, and one of the best, "Down the River with Henry Thoreau," in which you prove that no matter how many times the blurb-writers call you the Thoreau of the West, you are not Henry Thoreau. You take him with you—or at least his immortal remains in the form of *Walden*—on a trip down Utah's Green River. Sometimes you see through his eyes as you travel, but you also spend a fair amount of time arguing with him, getting peeved with him, occasionally allowing yourself moments of pity for him. What's worth taking from his thought and life, you take. What's worth admiring, you admire. But there's no blind admiration, no mindless aping (as more than a few of this generation have done). He goes with you down the river as a friend you want very much to understand, but also to come to terms with on *your* terms.

You understand, for example, that he found all the adventure he needed in his wanderings around Walden Pond and Concord. But still, no woman, no good beer, no pure love of the impurity of good food? No desire to join George Catlin in touring the great Western plains? Henry lived, you say, "an unnecessarily constrained existence, and not only in the 'generative' region."

He was, in other words, a puritan.

That's not Edward Abbey. Edward Abbey is closer to, say, D. H. Lawrence and his mockery of Ben Franklin's fear of "using venery" than he is to the continent sages of New England—though God only knows how you'll take *that* comparison. I have a notion that Lawrence's sex-sodden philosophies don't excite you much more than Thoreau's puritanism. There's not enough true adventure in either of them. "Though most of my mind and half my heart side with ... Thoreau," you say in the essay, "Fool's Treasure," "the rest belongs to the imbeciles. I, too, would have gone with the Forty-Niners. Who cares whether we found true gold or only fool's gold? The adventure lies in the search...." The search, the trip down all the rivers of thought and geography chasing the mystery of *la motif.*

And how constrained that makes Julio Cortázar and those like him sound, who prefer only "higher" experience, except perhaps when experience comes to venery. "Our job," you

say of yourself and your friend Debris, and I take it you also
mean other artists like yourselves, "is to record, each in his
own way, this world of light and shadow and time that will
never come again exactly as it is today." How sad if that world
is limited by urbane and urban puritans to a world of only
rooms, streets, raingutters.

You may be a purist—pure water, pure air, pure food, pure
honesty—but you'll gladly let the puritans hoist themselves
on their own petards, if puritans could bring themselves to
eat enough Abbey's Special Pinto Bean Sludge to admit to
petarding (petard: from vulg. Sp. *petardo*, "fart," an etymol-
ogy that I think would please you far more than it would
Henry).

And as for finding the abolition of time only in such "civilized" activities as the reading of Keats and Theocritus? You
can speak for yourself, Ed. "Each precious moment entails
every other. Each sacred place suggests the immanent presence of all places. Each man, each woman, exemplifies all humans. The bright faces of my companions, here, now, on this
Río Dolores, this River of Sorrows, somewhere in the melodramatic landscape of southwest Colorado, break my heart—
for in their faces, eyes, vivid bodies of action, I see the hope
and joy and tragedy of humanity everywhere. Just as the hermit thrush, singing its threnody back in the piney gloom of
the forest, speaks for the lost and voiceless everywhere.

"What am I trying to say? The same as before—everything. Nothing more than that. Everything implied by
water, motion, rivers, boats. By the flowing. . . ."

It is the *living* moment which truly abolishes time, that
eternal present tense which brings Heraclitus full circle for
you. The knowledge that you can't step into the same river
twice is far less important than the knowledge that in stepping into one river, you are in a sense stepping into all rivers,

with all people, through all time: "What matters is the strange, mysterious, overwhelming truth that *we* are *here now*, in this magnificent place, and never will know why. Or why not."

The participation in the mystery, the partnership of the now. Keats is one key to those. So is the Río Dolores.

Sometimes as I read *Down the River* and others of your books, I find myself fussing with you, gently fussing, as you fussed with Henry Thoreau, for all your admiration of him. (We've fussed face to face about a couple of these things, so I know there's no surprise for you here.) Not because of the contradictions I think you fall into from time to time: only the new puritans who infest us everywhere nowadays would have you, say, turn vegetarian, lie about liking venison (it's the *wanton* killing you hate, as did Thoreau). I've got nothing against mere contradictions: I'm told I've been guilty of one or two myself. Only math texts don't contradict themselves, and nobody ever picked up a math text to learn about life. Do you contradict yourself?—to steal the Whitman line. Then you contradict yourself. You are large. You contain multitudes. As we all do.

No, I fuss with you when you begin to romanticize the past of American Indians too much, for example, in the same book in which you write, in wondering about the lives of people who lived a hundred years ago in a Western mining town: "And where the work was hard, dangerous, the recreation crude and sometimes brutal, we might assume that those who lived here acquired personality traits adapted to their condition: a hardness of spirit, a relative indifference to suffering."

Yes, good point. Probably true.

Yet if it is true, what might we assume about a culture that hung babies from their feet in trees to teach them not to cry, that massacred their enemies in such exquisite ways (I know, I know, so did we), that took human scalps as trophies? To say that the American Indians' was a "bold, brave, heroic way of life, one as fine as anything recorded history has to show us," and let it go at that is a contradiction of a different color. If hard ways of life lead to a hardness of spirit, and a relative indifference to suffering, no race, no culture can be immune.

(As for the comment for which you've already taken enough flack: "The one thing we could do for a country like Mexico, for example, is to stop every illegal immigrant at the border, give him a good rifle and a case of ammunition, and send him home," because the alternative is "leaving our borders open to unlimited immigration until—and it won't take long—the social, political, economic life of the United States is reduced to the level of life in Juarez, Guadalajara, Mexico City, San Salvador, Haiti, India"—I won't add any flack. But give me a choice of living in Newark or Guadalajara, then go hide and watch how long it takes me to make up my mind.)

But when I'm done with my minor fussing, I'm back on the rivers with you, back in the mystery they represent to you. That notion of mystery is something you return to again and again, arguing with Bucky Fuller and Einstein about whether or not the earth and the universe are "comprehensible" in any sensible way. "A life full of wonder—wonderful," is what you're after, and you don't find that in any universe scientifically miniaturized into comprehensibility. "The most mysterious thing about the universe," you say in your superb essay about the windhover, "is not its comprehensibility but the fact that it exists. And the same mystery attaches to everything within it. The world is permeated through and through by mystery. By the incomprehensible. By creatures like you and me and Einstein and the lizards."

You're a watcher of the mystery, then, a watcher and a protector. Is there a better metaphor for what you do than the image of yourself living in a fire tower, doing your "job of watching," as you say in the same essay? "We watched the clouds again and the weather, and approaching and departing storms. We watched the sun go down behind Four Peaks and the Superstition Mountains, that sundown legend retold and recurring every evening, day after day. We saw the planet Venus bright as radium floating close to the shoulder of the new moon. We watched the stars, and meteor showers, and the snaky ripple of cloud-to-cloud lightning coursing across the sky at night. . . ."

"The forest spread below us in summer in seventeen different shades of green. There were yellow pine and piñon pine, blue spruce and Engelmann spruce, white fir and douglas fir, quaking aspen, New Mexican locust, alligator juniper, and four kinds of oak. Along the rimrock of the escarpment, where warm air rose from the canyons beneath, grew manzanita, agave, sotol, and several species of cactus—prickly pear, pincushion, fishhook. Far down in the canyons, where water flowed, though not always on the surface, we could see sycamore, alder, cottonwood, walnut, hackberry, wild cheery, and wild grape. And a hundred other kinds of tree, shrub, and vine that I would probably never learn to identify by name."

And Cortázar *complains* that a hill or a sunset are "the most recurrent things imaginable," pronounces ex cathedra that "you will never find a natural scene that can take more than five minutes of determined contemplation."

In language neither monosyllabic nor exclamatory, thus, thus you refute Julio Cortázar.

———

When you spot a fire, you report it, sometimes (if you can get to it) try to help put it out, as your political essays in aid of stopping needless nuclear power plants, dams, and other such perniciousness on the part of the technocrats, bureaucrats, and the rest of the rats show. That's part of getting down the river, too.

What counts is that you're a watcher *and* a participant. You go down into the woods and meet the bears. Philosophy naked always embarrasses you a little, though you can sit in the temple and argue with the best of them. But you can seldom allow yourself a flight of thought that you don't undercut soon after with Abbey wit or the admission of uncertainty, a "yes, but." (That's all right: Mark Twain would approve. Puncturing pomposity is an old American virtue threatened with extinction.) "Though a sucker for philosophy all of my life," you admit in "Meeting the Bear," "I am not a thinker but—a toucher. A *feeler*, groping his way with the white cane of the senses through the hairy jungle of life. I believe in nothing that I cannot touch, kiss, embrace— whether a woman, a child, a rock, a tree, a bear, a shaggy dog. The rest is hearsay. If God is not present in this young prickly pear jabbing its spines into my shin, then God will have to get by without my help. I'm sorry but that's the way I feel. The message in the bottle is not for me."

Which brings us back to Julio Cortázar, a great lover of messages in bottles. It's not that you don't respect those gifts of "civilization" that he so loves. I've seldom known a man with such a profound respect for books and writers as you— except those books and writers you suspect of nonsense, in which case you're murderous, as the reviews in *Down the River* make wickedly clear. No, the great difference in yourself and a man like Cortázar is that you leave room in the civilized universe for Theocritus *and* wild rivers—not to mention wild river rats.

That's what Cortázar is missing in what he's saying: those tacit definitions of his, those unquestioned assumptions. "Civilized people," for example. "Home."

Is Paris all there is to civilization? Is Buenos Aires? New York? Dear Lord, must a man as brilliant as Julio Cortázar blind himself just to prove he can walk with a cane?

"Wilderness complements and completes civilization," you answer. "I might say that the existence of wilderness is also a compliment to civilization. Any society that feels itself too poor to afford the preservation of wilderness is not worthy of the name of civilization." And in another place: "Civilization remains the ideal, an integrated realization of our intellectual, emotional, and physical gifts which humankind as a whole has nowhere yet attained."

Not even in Paris, Ed?

But "civilized people" will "curse the minute they left home to come and endure gnats, sunburn, and thorns," says Cortázar. Will they? Perhaps, if home means only a 2BR, LR, DR apartment with an as-it-were view, means no more than an easy chair and scotch at seven thirty (surprisingly, scotch and river water at seven thirty *is* considered a possibility by some moderately civilized people). But there is another kind of home to come home to. Here's how you define it: "'A man whose emotions are alive,' wrote Saul Bellow, 'is at home anywhere.' Now this may be true for an urbanite like Bellow, who has lived his life inside walls and under a roof; big cities, it's true, are pretty much the same everywhere. But a countryman has a place on earth that is his own, and much as he may love to wander, as I myself do, he loves the wandering more because he has a place to return to, a place where he belongs. A place to live and when his time comes, a place to die. The earth has fed me for half a century; I owe the earth a body. The debt shall be paid."

Deserts, mountains, woods, rivers. Places which *are* home to at least one civilized man.

Leaving Cortázar, breaking camp, back on the river. People who don't think much of you tell me there's an Abbey cult out here in the West, a kind of Abbeyanity that would make Aleister Crowley proud. I wouldn't know about that. If there is one, I'm not a member. Like Thoreau, I don't consider my-self a member of anything I didn't join, especially cults. I don't think you're a member either.

In fact, very likely the only rivers I'll ever go down with you, Ed, are these magic rivers of your books. (You do believe in magic, both good and bad—and you know the difference between magic and superstition.) In your introduction to *Down the River*, you tell the story of your first attempt to get out onto a river, the time you and your brother launched yourselves off in a heavy cement-mixing box and forthwith sank. Once when I was about the same age as you, I imagine, at the far southern end of those Appalachians into whose northern river you put your first *bateau ivre*, I launched my first one, also home made. The results were the same, and I imagine the impulse was pretty much the same, too. To chase *la motif*, go after the mystery 'round the bend. My grandfa-ther, I'm told, used to take off for weeks at a time and live alone in a cave on an Alabama river called the Black Warrior, eating only the fish he caught and maybe a few biscuits and beans he cooked up. When I was younger and things would get tough, I used to close my eyes and imagine that if things got tough enough, I could always find that cave.

I know now I can't. It's somewhere near the bottom of a

generic power-company lake that bears the generic name of
Smith. But I'm still stuck there. My own mysteries still live
there, in what's left of those slow, green Southern rivers my
mother had to row across to get to school, in the stillness of
their shadowy sloughs at the foot of those tree-heavy bluffs
where I first fell for rivers. I'll never get over that first love, I
imagine, a sucker for sentiment to the last. These noisy
Western rivers are a little too uppity and quick-tempered for
me. I'll stick with the deserts and the mountains and the
woods. And, forgive me River Spirits, swimming pools now
and again.

But for God's sake don't *you* stop going down your rivers,
either physical or metaphysical. I need those trips; *we* need
those trips, those of us who must forever be reminded what
it's like to "think like a mountain," but "feel like a river,"
who've become hopelessly addicted to sharing the magic and
the madness. Without those healing waters, where else
would we come to drink our antidotes to despair?

Un abrazo fuerte,
Bob

Joining the Visionary "Inhumanists"

I think I could turn and live with animals, they are so placid
  and self-contain'd,
I stand and look at them long and long.

They do not swear and whine about their condition,
They do not lie awake in the dark and weep for their sins,
They do not make me sick discussing their duty to God,
Not one is dissatisfied, not one is demented with the mania of
  owning things,
Not one kneels to another, nor to his kind that lived thousands
  of years ago,
Not one is respectable or unhappy over the whole earth.

                    Walt Whitman, "Song of Myself," Part 32

The term "inhumanist" is one coined by Robinson Jeffers to mean a person who rejects the philosophical tradition of the humanists, that tradition created in classical Greece which has dominated Western civilization, which sees all human endeavor as the central purpose of life, and in fact sees all life as having relative (and less) importance to human life and activity. But just as the American culture has spawned a new poetry, which really sees no need for classical metrical conventions and practices to make verse, it has also spawned a tradition growing out of both scientific awareness and rebellion against European civilization's domination, that says perhaps the human end is not really so important as we think. In Jeffers's poetry, much of it focused on the natural landscape of Carmel and Big Sur in central California, where he lived, the message is not only a cosmic one—the earth but a small part of the universe, and humans such an infinitely small part of the possibilities of life—but also a neo-Darwinian one in which humankind is a sort of evolutionary mistake, having turned into a murdering, raping, torturing, ravaging species which will certainly destroy itself while other life in the universe, perhaps even on the planet, will live on.

Even though the passage quoted above shows that possibility in Whitman, he is for the most part a true humanist who simply chooses to believe that all mankind *could* be filled with love if it would, and that slavery, war, and other ignominies will be wiped away when his bigger vision is obtained. Still, all the seeds of "inhumanism" are planted there in that vision, which does see man as pillaging rather than loving, and does idealize animals for at least not having the worst human vices. Jeffers, on the other hand, sees the human drama playing itself out, doomed and fascinating in its fated self-destruction. When Jeffers's editors at Random House in the forties finally realized what he was saying and were confronted by his antiwar politics in very specific terms, lumping Roosevelt, great American hero, along with Hitler and Mussolini, they not only censored some of the poems in *The Double Axe* (containing the long poem with one section entitled "The Inhumanist"), they wrote an editorial note, placed in the front of the book, disclaiming any of the ideas expressed in the book. The fear, not just patriotic or chauvinistic, of expressing a feeling that the human race was not the most important thing we could know, shocked everyone. This was not politics. It was an undermining of civilization.

Racing along under the surface of all of Ed Abbey's writing is that fiery "inhumanist" philosophy. It makes him love the desert above all things, but equally to have a desire to be in the wilderness anywhere, to explore and understand and simply be with the non-man, the a-human world. But pumping just as strong as a heart inside him is the tradition, his education, and his feeling that we must believe in human civilization, must try to save it, equivocating often to try to understand these contradictory urges in himself. In *Desert Solitaire*, near the end of Abbey's sojourn in Arches National Park as a ranger, on Labor Day weekend, a stranger who signs himself J. Prometheus Birdsong keeps him up all night discussing philosophy and what his real position is *vis à vis* the humanist issue. They decide that his only reason for arguing the humanist position at all is that he is human, and can't quite face the possibility that he is of no importance whatsoever. And in another discussion with this friend and fellow camper, Ralph Newcombe, he decides that he is not an atheist but an "earthiest." "Be true to the earth" is his motto. Yet it is this struggle with the human need to survive, triumph and continue in society and civilization, along with his feeling that humans are irrelevant to the cosmos, that makes Abbey's writing so rich. We are not being palmed off with nature-worship, nor are we being forced to see anything but the reality of 20th century man, who has immense resources and chronically uses them badly. At one point in *Desert Solitaire*, Abbey makes a distinction between "civilization" and "culture." Even though most of his examples are frivolous, the distinction is eminent in the argument for Abbey's aesthetic, which I think is neither Whitman's longing ("I stand and look at them long and long") for the world of humankind to be as free and pure of destructive vices, nor Jeffers's cynical belief that man is simply a mistake in evolution which the very process of evolution will soon make right and that war will simply destroy the planet.

Abbey is ultimately both politician and poet, spending half of his year in the wilderness, half in civilization, working for the Park Service and giving little programs of "revolution," as he calls them, by which we could set ourselves back on a constructive course. At the same time, he sees more and more the desert as a symbol for some ineffable greatness (God?), that it is in man's power to approach, perhaps contain. He says, "I am convinced now that the desert has no heart, that it presents a riddle which has no answer, and that the riddle itself is an illusion created by some limitation or exaggeration of the displaced human consciousness." And yet apparently for Abbey, the illusion is also that it does not matter whether one attains the answer, but whether one is allowed to continue the pursuit for it.

Strangely, Abbey is no prophet of doom. Like the desert, he seems to offer philosophies which do not bring final answers but lead one to other questions. The desert which is his passion is loved because it is one of the last things which no one could want to own. And even when it is temporarily co-opted for uranium ore or other precious minerals, it is always soon wasted again and finally left to the Abbeys of the world, those who do not want to own or exploit but only to be. He is eloquent on the need for wilderness on this planet. We need places where no one could choose to be, but because of that will be underdeveloped and thus be symbols of freedom. "The knowledge that refuge is available, when and if needed, makes the silent inferno of the desert more easily

bearable. Mountains complement desert as desert complements city, as wilderness complements and completes civilization.

"A man could be a lover and defender of the wilderness
without ever in his lifetime leaving the boundaries of as-
phalt, powerlines, and right-angled surfaces. We need wilderness whether or not we ever set foot in it. We need a
refuge even though we may never need to go there. I may
never in my life get to Alaska, for example, but I am grateful
that it's there. We need the possibility of escape as surely as
we need hope; without it the life of the cities would drive all
men into crime or drugs or psychoanalysis."

This vision of Abbey's is often co-opted for trendy and
fashionable uses, rather than used salvagingly as it might. For
Abbey, like Whitman and Jeffers, is trying to find a way to
understand his own humanness and failures while not doom-
ing the entire human race. But the inherent paradox in this
is unavoidable. In a rhapsodic passage near the beginning of
Desert Solitaire, he describes killing a rabbit with a stone, just
for the joy of being in the wilderness and being able to do it.
Not for meat, and not because he is actually a hunter. He is
trying to feel himself a part of the landscape. Yet, earlier that
same week he has had the problem of what to do about mice
in his trailer. They attract snakes, and he doesn't want to live
with rattlesnakes. He doesn't want to kill the mice. He
doesn't want either to have to kill the Faded Midget, a little
horned rattlesnake which has come to live under the steps.
Nature solves the problem for him, in one of the most
charming parts of *Desert Solitaire*, when Abbey tells the story
of his living with a bull snake for a few weeks, in April when
it's still cold. The snake loves the warm trailer and often curls
itself around Abbey's waist, inside his shirt. It drives away

both the Faded Midget from the doorstep and the mice. But Abbey deliberately sets up his wish not to kill, his humanist self—for the reader; then takes his walk into the desert where he savagely kills the rabbit for no reason at all:

> For a moment I am shocked at my deed; I stare at the quiet rabbit, his glazed eyes, his blood drying in the dust. Something vital is lacking. But shock is succeeded by a mild elation. Leaving my victim to the vultures and maggots, who will appreciate him more than I could—the flesh is probably infected with tularemia—I continue my walk with a new, augmented cheerfulness which is hard to understand but is unmistakable. What the rabbit has lost in energy and spirit seems added, by processes too subtle to fathom, to my own soul. I try but cannot feel any sense of guilt. I examine my soul: white as snow. Check my hands: not a trace of blood. No longer do I feel so isolated from the sparse and furtive life around me, a stranger from another world. I have entered into this one. We are kindred all of us, killer and victim, predator and prey, me and the sly coyote, the soaring buzzard, the elegant gopher snake, the trembling cottontail, the foul worms that feed on our entrails, all of them, all of us. Long live diversity, long live the earth!

What finally, then, is Abbey's vision?

Yes, we can say the Dionysian, in which we understand all of life to be part of a cycle, death as much a part of reality as birth, and death required before rebirth can occur. But why then the tirades against "culture" rather than "civilization," the anger against the motor vehicle, his hatred of all the tourists who come to the park? This seems to be different from Jeffers's "inhumanism" when looked at entirely; there is no real conviction here that all humanity is a mistake. If there is any political message constantly in Abbey's writings, it seems to be that we have overpopulated the world. Not that mankind is bad. Only that certain humans are, and that in large numbers humankind is trouble.

Is it specious to conclude that Abbey, like his Desert, presents riddles which have no answers? Perhaps. Yet maybe that is part of the appeal of his work in this time when we are aware of a very probably approaching nuclear holocaust. Perhaps his lack of doctrine or dogma is reassuring in itself:

> The desert says nothing. Completely passive, acted upon but never acting, the desert lies there like the bare skeleton of Being, spare, sparse, austere, utterly worthless, inviting not love but contemplation. In its simplicity and order it suggests the classical, except that the desert is a realm beyond the human and in the classical view only the human is regarded as significant or even recognized as real.

This meditative line, even though not the same as Jeffers's conclusions, is an "inhumanist" speculation. Certainly, it is what is beyond the human in the desert and wilderness which draws Abbey. And all of his readers must thank him, as we thank Whitman and Jeffers, for giving us some respite from our own resolutely self-centered, and probably destructive, humanism.

SAM HAMILL

Down the River Yin

A gray wind off the Pacific. The dark forests of Puget Sound are full of cedar and spruce and Doug fir. Here, a brief hundred years ago, native peoples carved out sea-going vessels from cedar trees that were saplings when Columbus was begging after boats. In Estonia, "Father Spruce" goes back four thousand years. Doug fir is commercial.

Gray skies the first day of May. Gray seas, gray gulls. But it's not the weather that makes me feel so gray. It's what Kawabata Yasunari called simply, "Beauty and sadness." How they fit together, how they compel. Because I have been re-reading Edward Abbey's *Down the River*, I have been remembering rivers—the Colorado River running beside Moab, Utah; the San Juan a little on south; the Novarro River south from Mendocino on the northern California coast where I first lived alone in an old Ford van, camping on "Timber Industry" land until they came in and fenced it all; and other rivers, in Alaska, British Columbia, Washington state, and in Japan.

Thinking of rivers on a gray day on Puget Sound, I remember the closing lines of a poem written by Li Yü nearly a thousand years ago:

> if you want to know the sum of human pain,
> watch the soft brown river rolling eastward in the spring.

Rivers often bring me to the edge of tears. Not just the damming of rivers, not just the foreseeable end to the salmon runs of these northwestern rivers, but something of the river itself. It reminds me also of a poem by Bashō:

> Not just my human sadness,
> hototogisu,
> but your solitary cry.

The hototogisu is the Japanese cuckoo. There is a resiliency in the clear perceptions of Kawabata, Li Yü, and Bashō that I have always found attractive. I mention this because these two Japanese and one Chinese gentlemen have been with me in much the same way that Mr. Abbey claims Thoreau (it's pronounced *thor*-ough, with the accent on the first syllable):

> I carry a worn and greasy paperback copy of a book called *Walden, or Life in the Woods.* Not for thirty years have I looked inside this book; now for the first time since my school days I shall.

Except that my greasy books are dog-eared from use. From Bashō's journey to the north, as from Tu Fu's, I have learned much that has shaped my mind and heart.

But Mr. Abbey makes claims for *Walden*'s author that trouble me. "I found that by working six weeks a year I could meet all the expenses of living," he quotes. Perhaps I am reading this wrong, but I can't help wondering what our Victorian amateur naturalist would do with the remaining 46 weeks of the year. And so forth.

There are moments in Thoreau's journals when I like him; there are wonderful passages on his Concord and Merrimac travels; but *Walden* is an ugly little book. Let me quote one of our finest literary journalists, Hayden Carruth, on *Walden:*

> That's what *Walden* is: a work conceived in rancor and composed in scorn. It is an elitist manifesto, a cranky, crabby dia-

tribe. Its victims are its readers, and none escapes. Its author
was sanctimonious, self-righteous, and ungenerous to the
point of cruelty. . . . At one point he tells how, when he was
walking along the railway, he saw a large toolbox, and "it suggested to me that every man who was hard pushed might get
such a one for a dollar, and, having bored a few auger holes in
it, to admit the air at least, get into it when it rained and at
night, and hook down the lid, and so have freedom in his
love, and in his soul be free." His very words: "freedom in
his love"—in a box! So Thoreau solves the problem of sex by
masturbation, and the problems of all humanity by isolation.

One cannot but wonder whether Thoreau's box served at
some point as inspiration for Samuel Beckett's garbage cans.
For Thoreau is a moral cripple. For all the beautiful things
he said, for all his proclamations about preferring truth to
imagination and so forth, he was a man without compassion.
He was also a man who had no woman for a friend. On nearly
every page of *Walden* one finds a spiritual violence combined
with chaotic declarations of self-esteem. "I'm a *real* humanist," Mr. Abbey asserts. "I'd sooner shoot a man than a
snake."

But I've been told again and again that Mr. Abbey's declarations of violent intent aren't meant to be taken literally.
But, if that is true, just how *are* we to take them?

The ancient Chinese believed (and I believe) that our essential nature is still. And that compassion is the foundation
of wisdom. Kung-fu tse says all wisdom is rooted in learning
to call things by the right name. What is missing in *Walden* is
sometimes missing in Mr. Abbey's appreciation of that book:
restraint. It is too easy to appeal to what is base in human
character, to gain popularity by saying what the audience
wants to hear. It is too easy to recommend *Walden* without
reservation.

Some years back, Gary Snyder told me a story. It seems

there was to be an ecology teach-in or some such thing. Mr. Snyder, at his own expense I understand, printed a few hundred copies of an essay he'd written ("Four Changes," if memory serves), and sent them off to the get-together because his own schedule didn't permit his attendance. He sent the essays to Mr. Abbey to pass on to the participants. After no word for some time, Mr. Snyder wrote to ask, "Did you get the essay? Did you pass it out? What did you think?" And the answer came back: "Got the essay. Passed it out. I liked it, except for the Buddhist bullshit."

Hearing this story from a man who has been a devout student of Buddhism for many, many years, it is funny and enlightening. But when Mr. Abbey tells the tale, it begins to have an element of rancor, a smug, self-serving note not at all disharmonious with the tone of *Walden*.

Looking for the stillness at the center of things. And Olson's refrain comes back: I have had to learn the simplest things last. Which made for difficulties.

Calling things by the right names, one's self comes into order. Because one's self is orderly, order comes into the house; because the home is orderly, order comes into the neighborhood; because the community is orderly, order is brought to the state. From the Prince of Heaven down to the commonest of the common, self-discipline is the root.

Mr. Abbey imagines a honeymoon with Henry David married to Emily Dickinson.

She: (raising her pen) Henry, you haven't taken out the garbage.

He: (raising his flute) Take it out yourself.

> If you cannot recognize the order within you, how do you expect to understand the natural order around you?
>
> *Shimaboku Eizo*

Sitting at my desk, looking out at the forest behind the row of houses at this former Army fort, I see a hawk circling, moving slowly and steadily southwest, circling. And I can remember back to the framing of my small house, a few friends dropped by to help. And Ernie Baird would suddenly say quickly, "Hawk!" And we would stop and watch, saying nothing because there was nothing to say, because saying nothing said it all. Silence is, I believe, the highest form of moral superiority. Not in the sense of Mr. Thoreau, but in the sense of meditation, in the way Jesus stood in his silence before asking, "Thou sayest it."

And now the hawk is gone over the trees, over the gray waters of the Pacific northwest, into the darkest corners of the human heart.

And what is left is not even memory, only the vaguest notion of a knowledge that inhabits, perhaps, the gene pool itself—the *feel* of natural order Mr. Abbey has so eloquently articulated in *Desert Solitaire*, *The Journey Home*, *Abbey's Road*, and elsewhere.

But in this Taoist-Buddhist-Confucian view of things, where is there room for invective? We have elected a government which, following the wishes of the People, has made us little-loved as we have ever been in this world. And what invective will stand out against Holocaust, against the sound of the MX missile, against the ultimate nuclear nightmare—what name-calling can possibly help us recover from our own suicidal impulse?

In a perversion of Confucian reason, the Pentagon declares that the construction of MX missiles will help business; business, in turn, will require more employees, and all of this will, of course, help to bring the nation into economic equilibrium. Contemplating the 24,000-year half-life of plutonium 239, Mr. Abbey drinks beer. This is invective of the highest order, a gentle nose-thumbing at international stupidity that would earn a small smile from Tu Fu or Kung-fu tse. This is the *wu-wei*, action through non-action. The sort of restraint one admires when one remembers another military headquarters that promised work would make us free.

"He says that woman speaks with nature. That she hears voices from under the earth. That wind blows through her ears and trees whisper to her. That the dead sing through her mouth and the cries of infants are clear to her. But for him this dialogue is over. He says he is not part of this world, that he was set on this world as a stranger. He sets himself apart from woman and nature." This is the opening paragraph of Susan Griffin's *Woman and Nature.* Two hundred pages later, Susan Griffin says, speaking of her sister, Earth: "I do not forget: what she is to me, what I am to her."

And I think: I would like to eavesdrop on a dialogue between Edward Abbey and Susan Griffin.

In Mr. Abbey's books, men are men. They drink beer and float rivers and sweat and piss in parking lots and cuss like a bunch of good old boys on a binge in the desert. I suspect they are a little lonely. Because there aren't many women around.

And I think that most of our men are like that. Because they've alienated themselves from the domicile. A hundred years ago, the home was the major point of manufacture in the civilized as well as primitive world. We have sought *wyf-dom* as a form of exploiting indentured servantry. We have forgotten the true meaning of husbandry.

That unpleasant fellow, Henry David, won't take the garbage out. He is miserable and reclusive not because he so loves "nature," but because he is alienated from the essential duties of being alive.

I wonder what kind of *stuff* Mr. Thoreau dumped in that pond.

He'd probably shudder to hear another old geezer in gray whiskers say it, but I love Edward Abbey. He's a high-class quarrel. While every pseudo-eco-freak in the country is toasting tofu, he's off with a beer pissing vinegar into the fuel tank of a D-8 Cat.   .

He cuts a singular trail, teetering on the brink of hypocrisy. He commits a good-natured heresy.

I'd like to buy him a beer. And ask a few questions about his home. Like who is his wife. How many kids has he had. How many ex-wives. I'd like to talk about population, commitment, balance in personal affairs.

Because I love Edward Abbey, and because I'm a *real* feminist, I'd rather quarrel with him than shoot him.

Because I love Edward Abbey's books, I have committed this heresy, I have raised some issues that have been nagging me through many of his books for many years. I do so because I'm certain that the praise for his achievement will be fulsome. And because I'm sure he won't mind. Except for the Confucian bullshit. And the feminist bullshit. And the Taoist.

And that's fine. Perhaps some day we will meet and share a jug of wine on the banks of the River Yin.

GARY SNYDER

A Letter to Ed Abbey

Dear Ed,

You know, the reason that we never had further correspondence (I guess) was not—as you suggest in the book—
because of any comments about Buddhism, but just because
it didn't happen. So it does happen that I write you now,
though again, curiously enough, on the point of Buddhism.
George Sessions forwarded me some of the questions from
the letter you wrote him 22:VIII:82 suggesting I might want
to deal with them, and I might as well.

The bad rap that has been put on India and the Far Eastern cultures, by half-baked historical information, is hard
to undo. It's a matter, I suppose, of getting out of Utah or
Arizona grooves, as much as us on the coast getting out of
"California" grooves. What I have to address first is your
statement that these are the "most miserable, most abused,
most man-centered cultures on earth." I don't know where
you got that notion. India, of course, is a totally different culture, and essentially an occidental culture, as against the Far
East. The Himalayas, the drainages of the Irrawaddy, the
Sutlej and the impenetrable mountains of Yunnan separate
the Far East from India. Also there are the little matters of
total racial difference and total linguistic family difference.
India has been, it's true, a nation with considerable problems

for the last few centuries. Many of these problems were brought about by the deliberate policies of England, who for some decades dumped textiles in India until the local weaving industry collapsed and then sold Manchester goods at an elevated price to a captive consumer audience. There are studies on how Europe impoverished the rest of the world. Just because they are by Marxists, I wouldn't necessarily slight them. Like Mexico by the Spaniards, India was encouraged in many ways to give up its local sustainability. You might know that opium was developed by British industry as a crop in Nepal in the low-lying areas, and then to guarantee that there was a market for it, Britain shoved opium down the throats of the Chinese population. This was called the "opium war." China, your purgatory, has not yet forgotten the injustice and indignity of having drug addiction forced on it by the West.

But to go on: India has an average population density of about forty to sixty persons to the square mile, as I recall, which is about that of Hungary or Czechoslovakia. It is not particularly densely populated—especially compared to Belgium, or Java. It had up through the Gupta period one of the most affluent civilizations on earth—a lot of it went down through a combination of goats and deforestation. The goats, of course, eat the reproduction. Soil erosion, deforestation, sheep and goats, as economic devices of agrarian societies are not the invention of Hinduism or Buddhism. From the Neolithic onward, these are domesticates that have been part of agrarian economies everywhere. I dare say you are aware of the fact that Greece and much of Italy once were covered by pine and oak forests, with fine pastures and springs, and the present chaparral brush of most of the Mediterranean in no way represents the plant communities of early historic times. This also was deforestation and goats.

We could just as well attribute the deterioration of early civilized environments, then, to democratic Athenian orators, as we could to these sick oriental religions.

The great early Indian king Ashoka was one of the few world leaders, to my knowledge, who actually went so much against the grain of the dynamics of agrarian states as to have carved on rock instructions about not taking the life of animals, and of compassion for non-human beings. The "rock edicts of Ashoka."

Even with the problems that India has had, though, and still has, it strikes me that it's remarkable how hard the villagers try to keep their patience and keep in tune with wild nature. Articles on attacks on villagers by tigers in the Nepal Terai remark on how many months or years it will be that village people tolerate the occasional death of one of their members on account of some elderly, ailing tiger, before they finally go to the government hunter for help. Situations where an American or probably European population would immediately form a posse with five hundred .300 rifles and jeeps are totally different. In my own travels in India, as well as studies, I was deeply impressed by the interpenetration of bird and animal species with the agricultural areas. The environmental disruptions of India are probably little worse than those of, say, Italy, Sicily, or much of Greece. The mountains at the headwaters of the Adriatic were once covered with marvelous forests; they disappeared to keep supplying the Roman fleet.

China is much the same case: though forests and soils have suffered greatly in the lower watersheds of the Yangtse and the Yellow, western Chinese mountains and the mountains of northern Siberia are still well forested. As with India, China was for a spell one of the most splendidly civilized and wealthiest countries on earth. Their cultural high point was probably the thirteenth century; when they were on the edge of great literacy, inexpensive editions of encyclopedias of all kinds of learning were available to the public, sophisticated instruments such as letters of credit were making the economy seem virtually modern, and a number of Buddhist and philosophical schools enjoyed great debate with each other. The century of violent Mongol rule helped bring an end to all that.

As for Japan, if you have been there, I suspect it has been only to Tokyo and the strip down to Osaka. It is certainly technologically busy, but it is also a culture which still knows how to relax, play, and enjoy great conviviality. Every time I visit Japan, I am struck by how gracefully they deal with their crowdedness, and how well they are able to enjoy life in inexpensive ways. The back-country from the major cities is astonishingly green and natural. Agriculture runs out the shoestring valleys, but climb any Japanese hill and you look out upon mile upon mile of forested mountains. When I was living in Kyoto, the newspaper reported much sighting of bears only twelve miles north of town. A city of three million. The last bear became extinct in England in the thirteenth century. Japan, a country of much larger population and about the same size as England, still has bear, wildcat, foxes, little mountain goats called kamo, deer, monkeys, and a host of other animals from their original days, still not too far off in the woods. The northern island of Hokkaido—which has again an average population of about sixty people per square mile, the same as Czechoslovakia—has an estimated population of three thousand giant brown bears (relatives of the grizzly and the kodiak). Not to mention a huge deer population. The reluctance of Japanese people to go on punitive expeditions against marauding wild pigs, etc., again is a striking contrast to the ways of westerners.

I have tried to describe a little what I think the actual conditions in these countries are. Certainly, human numbers and human greed have done little worse here than they have in other parts of the world: if anything is to blame, it is the nature of that type of social organization we call "civilization" itself—kingship, ruling elites, and the accumulation of wealth. Buddhism (which incidentally does not teach that everything is "illusion" but teaches that the way people see through their self-centered personal interest rosy glasses of subjectivity is "delusive"—and teaches people to see the world "as it is" which is the "real world" rather than the "illusory world" of subjective opinion) has not had a great deal of influence on the civilizations it coexisted with, it's true. Such teachings are never terribly successful on a large scale in any civilization, because they truly run against the grain. Philosophically, early Buddhism is closer to pre-Socratic Greek philosophy than anything else probably. Still, though Buddhism did not make so wonderful an impact, its truth and validity remains and I am grateful for the fact that it tempered medieval north India, Tibet, China, Korea, Japan, Mongolia, Burma and Thailand, in its attitudes at least toward taking life to the extent that people in those realms still are tender-hearted toward birds, animals, and trees. There have probably been other worthwhile by-products of the Buddhist presence in the Far East—architecture and art, cooking, manners, poetry and drama, a few little touches. You see, I look on the usefulness of Buddhism as in some ways just beginning now: though its very survival up till now is a marvel. Inside the Zen tradition there has been kept alive a person-to-person mode of actual body-and-mind-training (in the matter of purging one's self of subjectivity) that is extraordinary, in the face of normal history. I won't argue any further as to what I think the virtues of Buddhism might be

for the future—a non-anthropocentric species-wide compassion has value of its own.

I don't know what American Zen Buddhist types you have
seen. There are all sorts, but if you were to take one example—the San Francisco Zen Center—and its impact on the
community, you'd notice that it works in the world with
good baking (the bakery); good cooking (the "Greens" restaurant); good sewing (the stitchery); good manners, good
donation of good volunteer labor to good projects, a little
good art, much good humor, some peace activism via the
Buddhist Peace Fellowship, and lots of people who are doing
no harm at the very least.

Thinking back on what I've just written, in response to
your notions about Asia, I swear it's like you had exactly the
same view of Buddhism and China as my Texas Methodist
aunt. Stereotypes die hard.

But onward: To comradeship, and the work that must be
done. I think a grand mix of environmental religions is just
fine, if it does no harm, and I welcome neo-shamanists,
mother-goddess worshipers, neo-pagans, and whatever else
to the scene if that helps them get the energy to go to work
against industrial civilization. Even Marxists! (I forgot to
say: I really can't accept China as quite the purgatory you describe it. It was pretty bad through the Cultural Revolution,
but they seem to be doing quite well now, with no self-
deception—a billion people, and they know they are just
barely scrabbling by, trying to make it work. I met with eight
writers from the People's Republic three weeks ago in L.A.,
and was struck by their honesty, humility, and sense of the
enormity of the task of sheer survival ahead of them. They
are serious about birth control.)

So, let's get together under the general name of Deep
Ecology and roust out the troops. I loved *The Monkey Wrench*

Gang, me and my boy laughed all the way through it. So in
the letter I wrote Dave Foreman I was not knocking *The
Monkey Wrench Gang* as literature, or theater, or device, but
as you know, questioning how we want to handle, seriously,
the point of possible violence in the movement. I stand by
what I said there—we need warriors, not rhetoricians. And
anybody who is truly intent on radical action doesn't go
shooting their mouth off about it, like some of those guys do.
But I love their energy and consider myself essentially in the
same boat. I hope you consider me in your boat as I consider
you in my boat, and hope we can walk some ridge or canyon
together somewhere sometime; if you are coming to California let me know and we'll get together up here at my place
and get George up here too—

> Fraternally,
> Gary

Abbey's Road

Edward Abbey, who died in March 1989, at sixty-two, seemed, at his best, like the nonpareil "nature writer" of recent decades. It was a term he came to detest, a term used to pigeonhole and marginalize some of the more intriguing American writers alive, who are dealing with matters central to us, yet it can be a ticket to oblivion in the review media. Joyce Carol Oates, for instance, in a slapdash though interesting essay called "Against Nature," speaks of nature writers' "painfully limited set of responses . . . REVERENCE, AWE, PIETY, MYSTICAL ONENESS." She must never have read Mr. Abbey; yet it was characteristic of him that for an hour or two, he might have agreed.

He wrote with exceptional exactitude and an uncommonly honest and logical understanding of causes and consequences, but he also loved argument, churlishness, and exaggeration. Personally, he was a labyrinth of anger and generosity, shy but arresting because of his mixture of hillbilly with cowboy qualities, and even when silent, appeared bigger than life. He had hitchhiked west from Appalachia for the first time at seventeen, for what became an immediate love match, and, I'm sure, slept out more nights under the stars than all of his current competitors combined. He was uneven, self-indulgent as a writer, and sometimes scanted his talent by working too fast. But he had about him an authenticity that springs from the page and is beloved by a rising generation of readers who have enabled his early collection of rambles, *Desert Solitaire* (1968), to run through eighteen printings in mass-market paperback and his fine comic novel, *The Monkey Wrench Gang* (1975), to sell half a million copies. Both books, indeed, have inspired a new eco-guerrilla environmental organization called Earth First!, whose other patron saint is Ned Ludd (from whom the Luddites took their name), though it's perhaps no more radical than John Muir's Sierra Club appeared to be in 1892, when that group was formed.

Like many good writers, Abbey dreamed of producing "The Fat Masterpiece," as he called the "nuvvle" he had worked on for the last dozen years, which was supposed to boil everything down to a thousand pages. When edited in half, it came out in 1988 as *The Fool's Progress*, an autobiographical yarn that lunges cross-country several times, full of apt descriptions and antic fun—*Ginger Man* stuff— though not with the coherence or poignancy he had hoped for. A couple of his other novels hold up fairly well too: *Black Sun* and *The Brave Cowboy*, which came out in movie form, starring Kirk Douglas and Walter Mattheau, in 1962 (*Lonely Are the Brave*) and brought Abbey a munificent $7,500.

I do think he wrote masterpieces, but they were more slender: the essays in *Desert Solitaire* and an equivalent sampler that you might put together from subsequent collections like *Down the River, Beyond the Wall,* and *The Journey Home.* His rarest strength was in being concise, because he really knew what he thought and cared for. He loved the desert—"red mountains like mangled iron"—liked people in smallish clusters, and didn't mince words in saying that industrial rapine, glitz malls, and tract sprawl were an abomination heralding more devastating events. While writing as hand-somely as others do, he never lost sight of the fact that much of Creation is rapidly being destroyed. "Growth for the sake of growth is the ideology of the cancer cell," he wrote. And he adopted for a motto Walt Whitman's line: "Resist much, obey little." Another was Thoreau's summary in *Walden:* "If I repent of anything, it is very likely to be my good behavior. What demon possessed me that I behaved so well?"

Abbey traveled less than some writers do, but it is not nec-essary to go dithering around our suffering planet, visiting the Amazon, Indonesia, Bhutan, and East Africa. The crisis is plain in anyone's neck of the woods, and the exoticism of globe-trotting may only blur one's vision. Nor do we need to become mystical Transcendentalists and commune with God. ("One Life at a Time, Please" is another of Abbey's ti-tles. On his hundreds of camping trips he tended to observe and enjoy the wilds rather than submerge his soul.) What is needed is honesty, a pair of eyes, and a further dollop of forti-tude to spit the truth out, not genuflecting to "Emersonian" optimism, or journalistic traditions of staying deadpan, or the saccharine pressures of magazine editors who want their readers to feel good. Emerson would be roaring with heart-break and Thoreau would be raging with grief in these 1990s. *Where were you when the world burned? Get mad, for a change, for heaven's sake!* I believe they would say to milder col-leagues.

Abbey didn't sell to the big book clubs or reach best-sellerdom or collect major prizes. When, at sixty, he was of-fered a smallish one by the American Academy of Arts and Letters, he rejected it with a fanfare of rhetoric, probably be-cause it had come too late. War-horse that he was, he did not find a ready market in mainstream publications of any stripe and was relegated through most of his career by the publicity arm of publishing to the death trap of "naturalist" stuff. So the success, wholly word-of-mouth, of *The Monkey Wrench Gang* in paperback pleased him more than anything else, and he delighted in telling friends who the real-life counterparts were for its characters, Seldom Seen Smith, Bonnie Abbzug, and George Washington Hayduke. They, too, had torn down billboards, yanked up survey stakes, poured sand into bulldozer gas tanks, and sabotaged "certain monstrosities" in fragilely scenic regions that shouldn't need freelance protection in the first place, as "Seldom Seen" says, still taciturn now, when you call him up.

"Abbzug" speaks of how Abbey in real life would go through three (used) cars a year, bouncing across the Sonoran Desert on his pleasure jaunts, peeling the plates off of each as it died. And when they got fooling, he would laugh till he had to come up for air, then laugh some more, even once when they'd broken down a great many miles from water and thought they were doomed, with only a bottle of wine to live on. Most good writers are walkers, but Abbey was something different, ranging the Southwest afoot or river running with somewhat the scope of John Muir in the High Sierras. It was the building of Hetch Hetchy Dam in Yosemite National Park (now thought to have been unnecessary for San Francisco's water needs) that finally embittered Muir; and the unfinished business of "monkeywrenching" in *The Monkey Wrench Gang* is to blow up Glen Canyon Dam, a structure that, before Abbey's eyes, had drowned a whole stretch of the Colorado River's most pristine, precious canyons.

Robinson Jeffers, another regionalist of fluctuating popularity, who made the close examination of his home country at Big Sur in California a prism to look at the rest of the world, concluded in several poems that mankind had turned

into "a sick microbe," a "deformed ape," "a botched experi-
ment that has run wild and ought to be stopped." In "The
Broken Balance" (1929) he spoke for Abbey's anger as well:

> The beautiful places killed like rabbits to make a city,
> The spreading fungus, the slime-threads
> And spores . . . I remember the farther
> Future, and the last man dying
> Without succession under the confident eyes of the stars.

"Let's keep things the way they were," Abbey liked to say.
Yet he was a bold, complex man who had had five wives and
five children by the end of his life; and although he spilled
too much energy into feuds with his allies and friends, he was
often a jubilant writer, a regular gleeman, not just a threno-
dist, and wanted to be remembered as a writer of "that letter
which is never finished"—literature—such as *Desert Solitaire* is.

We corresponded occasionally for twenty years, wanting
to go for a lengthy sail on the Sea of Cortez or go camping
somewhere in the hundred-mile Air Force gunnery range
which for its isolation eventually became another favorite re-
doubt of his. I hoped we could drift down the Yukon River
together and compile a dual diary. ("Is that dual or *duel*?" he
asked once.) He had lived in Hoboken, New Jersey, for a couple of years while unhappily married, with the "Vampire
State Building" on the skyline—also in Scotland and Italy—
and responded to Manhattan's incomparably gaudy parade
of faces as a cosmopolitan, though marked, himself, as an
outlander by his uncut grayish beard, slow speech, earnest
eyes, red-dog road shuffle, raw height and build, and jean
jacket or shabby brown tweed. On his way home to Oracle,
Arizona, he'd usually stop in the Alleghenies, after confer-
ring in New York City with editors, to visit his mother, Mil-

dred, a Woman's Christian Temperature Union veteran, and his father, Paul Revere Abbey, a registered Socialist and old Wobbly organizer, who'd met Eugene V. Debs in his youth and has toured Cuba and still cuts hickory fence posts in the woods for a living.

Abbey was a writer who liked to play poker with cowboys, while continuing to ridicule the ranch owners who over-graze the West's ravaged grasslands. The memorial picnic for him in Saguaro National Monument outside Tucson went on for twelve hours; and besides readings performed with rock-bottom affection, there was beer drinking, love-making, gunfire, and music, much as he had hoped. The pot-luck stew was from two "slow elk," as he liked to call beef cattle poached from particularly greedy entrepreneurs on the public's wildlands. He was an "egalitarian," he said—by which he meant that all wildlife and the full panoply of natu-ral vegetation have a right to live equal to man's—and these beeves had belonged to a cowman who specialized in hound-ing Arizona's scarce mountain lions.

Abbey died of internal bleeding from a circulatory disor-der, with a few weeks' notice of how sick he was. Two days before the event, he decided to leave the hospital, wishing to die in the desert, and at sunup had himself disconnected from the tubes and machinery. His wife, Clarke, and three friends drove him out of town as far as his condition allowed. They built a campfire for him to look at, until, feeling death at hand, he crawled into his sleeping bag with Clarke. But by noon, finding he was still alive and possibly better, he asked to be taken home and placed on a mattress on the floor of his writing cabin. There he said his gentle goodbyes.

His written instructions were that he should be "trans-ported in the bed of a pickup truck" deep into the desert and buried anonymously, wrapped in his sleeping bag, in a beautiful spot where his grave would never be found, with "lots of rocks" piled on top to keep the coyotes off. Abbey of course loved coyotes (and, for that matter, buzzards) and had played the flute to answer their howls during the many years he had earned his living watching for fires from government towers on the Grand Canyon's North Rim, on Aztec Peak in Tonto National Forest, and in Glacier National Park, before he finally won tenure as a "Fool Professor" at the University of Arizona. His friend who was the model for G. W. Hayduke in *The Monkey Wrench Gang* was squatting beside him on the floor as his life ebbed away—"Hayduke," under a real-life name, is a legend in his own right in parts of the West, a contemporary mountain man who returned to Tucson as to a "calving ground" several years ago when he wanted to have children—and the last smile that crossed Abbey's face was when "Hayduke" told him where he would be put.

The place is, inevitably, a location where mountain lions, antelope, bighorn sheep, deer, and javelinas leave tracks, where owls, poor-wills, and coyotes hoot, rattlesnakes crawl, and cacomistles scratch, with a range of stiff terrain overhead, and greasewood, rabbitbush, ocotillo, and noble old cactuses about. First seven, then ten buzzards gathered while the grave was being dug; but, as he had wished, it *was* a rocky spot. "Hayduke" jumped into the hole to be sure it felt O.K. before laying Abbey in, and afterward, in a kind of reprise of the antic spirit that animates *The Monkey Wrench Gang* (and that should make anybody but a developer laugh out loud), went around heaping up false rock piles at ideal grave sites throughout the Southwest, because this last peaceful act of outlawry on Abbey's part was the gesture of legend, and there will be seekers for years.

The stuff of legend: like Thoreau's serene passage from life muttering the words "moose" and "Indian," and Muir's thousand-mile walks to Georgia, or in the Sierras, "the Range of Light." Can he be compared to them? Muir, after all, bullied the Catskills naturalist John Burroughs from sheer orneriness, as Abbey, the controversialist, regularly blistered his colleagues with vitriol through the mails, and Thoreau—a stark individual in his own way—orated vehemently on behalf of the reviled "terrorist" John Brown. (That Thoreau of witticisms such as what a pearl was: "the hardened tear of a diseased clam, murdered in its old age.") A magazine published Abbey's last account of a trip by horseback through Utah's slick-rock canyons, and it's got a hop like a knuckleball's on it, unmistakably Abbey, as briny with personality as his heyday essays. Nor had twenty years changed him. Thoreau, by contrast, in a swift incandescent burst of work, vaulted from the relatively conventional *Week on the Concord and Merrimack Rivers* to the vision of *Walden*, but soon fell back into dutiful natural science. And Muir went from being a lone-wolf botanist and geologist to a passionate advocate, skillfully lobbying Teddy Roosevelt and William Howard Taft on behalf of Yosemite National Park, until, late in life, when he was finished with localism, he wandered rather disconsolately to Africa, Asia, and South America in celebrity guise.

Abbey was consistent but, unlike Thoreau, was not self-contained; some compulsive agenda unknown to him blunted his efforts to surpass himself. And his ambitions were confined to truth telling, rhapsody, and the lambasting of villains. As an essayist he did not aspire to the grandeur of versatility, or try hard to turn into a man of letters either— his novels can seem flat or foreshortened next to Peter Matthiessen's, for example, and his literary pronouncements were scattershot, bilious, or cursory. Like most conservationists, he was a political radical but a social conservative, going so far as to aver the old-fashioned idea that there are two sexes, not simply one, which, expressed with his customary crowing, abrasive overstatement, offended people. (Yet he wrote in a love letter to a woman friend after a breakup, "If you ever need me in any way I will cross continents and oceans to help you," a sentiment that even his favorite *bête noire*, Gloria Steinem, might have appreciated.) Speaking of various sins of omission of his personal life, he would sometimes describe himself as a coward—as being a neglectful father to his sons and a passive witness to his second wife's death by cancer, in particular.

There's a saying that life gets better once you have outlived the bastards, which would certainly be true except that as you do, you are also outliving your friends. I miss him. Sitting in silence in restaurants as our twinned melancholy groped for expression, or talking with him of hoodoo stone pillars and red-rock canyons, I've seldom felt closer to anybody. Honesty is a key to essay writing: not just "a room of one's own" but a view of one's own. The lack of it sinks more talented people into chatterbox hackwork than anything else. And Abbey aspired to speak for himself in all honesty—*X: His Mark*—and died telling friends he had done what he could and was ready. He didn't buzz off to Antarctica or the Galápagos Islands, yet no one will ever wonder what he really saw as the world burned. He said it; didn't sweeten it or blink at it or water it down or hope the web of catastrophes might just go away. He felt homesick for the desert when he went to Alaska, and turned back, yet if you travel much there, it is Abbey's words you will see tacked on the wall again and again in remote homestead cabins in the Brooks Range or in offices in Juneau, because he had already written of greed, of human brutality and howling despair, better than writers who write books on Alaska.

Last year a paean to Abbey's work in *National Review* finished with a quote from a passage in Faulkner: "*Oleh, Chief. Grandfather.*" To which we can add Amen. But instead let's close with a bit of Ed Abbey, from a minor book called *Appalachian Wilderness* (1970), which foretold why he chose that lost grave where he lies:

> How strange and wonderful is our home, our earth, with its swirling vaporous atmosphere, its flowing and frozen liquids, its trembling plants, its creeping, crawling, climbing creatures, the croaking things with wings that hang on rocks and soar through fog, the furry grass, the scaly seas . . . how utterly rich and wild. . . . Yet some among us have the nerve, the insolence, the brass, the gall to whine about the limitations of our earthbound fate and yearn for some more perfect world beyond the sky. We are none of us good enough for the world we have.

A Eulogy for Edward Abbey

Arches National Park
May 20, 1989

We are a family, a tribe, a clan, flocked together at a full moon in May, on slickrock. We have made a pilgrimage to the center of the universe, Abbey's country. Things are different now. Edward Abbey is gone. We know the physical fact of these words and we grieve. We know the spiritual truth of the words and we smile. Ed is here and will always be. His words reverberate on canyon walls, his voice being carried by desert winds on the open skies of the American West. He is Coyote, a dance upon the desert.

Edward Abbey didn't have to die to find paradise. He understood and lived it here and now. His words:

> When I write paradise, I mean not apple trees and only golden women, but also scorpions and tarantulas and flies, rattlesnakes and gila monsters, sandstone, volcanos, and earthquakes, bacteria, bear, cactus, yucca, bladderweed, oco-tillo and mesquite, flash floods and quicksand, and yes, dis-ease and death and the rotting of flesh. Paradise is the here and now, the actual, tangible dogmatically real Earth on which we stand. Yes, God bless America, the Earth upon which we stand.

Abbey knew we had it all right here, right now, we need
not look farther, we need not go further. Ed's death lay on
surfaces. His words:

> For my own part, I am pleased enough with surfaces. In fact,
> they alone seem to be of much importance. Such things for
> example as the grasp of a child's hand in your own, the flavor
> of an apple, the embrace of a friend or lover, the silk of a girl's
> thigh, the sunlight on rock and leaves, the feel of music, the
> bark of a tree, the abrasion of granite and sand, the plunge of
> clear water into a pool, the face of the wind, what else is there,
> what else do we need?

Perhaps there is one thing—I believe Ed knew and understood the art, the practice, of keeping in touch. The simple
act of correspondence. Familiar? One white, generic post-
card from Wolf's Hole, from Oracle, from Moab, Utah.
Signed always, "Love, Ed." Think about the thousands of
postcards with Abbey's words, his scribblings that have
crossed these lands, these sacred lands like a blizzard, like migrating birds, like shooting stars, U.S. Mail, Abbey's courier,
keeping in touch.

I first received mine in October 1979. It read simply:
"Nice meeting you in Salt Lake City, Tempest. Come to
Tucson. I would like to show you around the desert. Love,
Ed." The cards kept coming over the years, not often, but
consistently. Small exchanges back and forth, simple jot-
tings, a dialogue of news as well as ideas, keeping in touch.

A couple of autumns ago, September 1987, to be exact, Ed
did show me the desert. Not in Tucson, but in Utah. His
heartland, my homeland. We met in Moab; we spent the day
in Millcreek Canyon. A simple meander through slickrock.
I hear his voice ahead of me as we descend into the canyon,

dropping from ledge to ledge: "What most humans really desire is really something quite different from industrial gimmickry—liberty, spontaneity, nakedness, mystery, wildness, wilderness." A Coors six-pack carton had lodged itself behind a bitterbrush. Abbey kicked it, bent down, set it on fire, kept walking. I hear his words: "What we need now are heroes and heroines, about a million of them, one brave deed is worth a thousand books. Sentiment without action is the ruin of the soul." We descend further into the canyon, jump a few more ledges. My confidence had been lost a few months earlier in a fall in Blacksteer Canyon, now called "Bumsteer Canyon." Eighty stitches running down the center of my forehead like a river. "So I hear you're trying to etch the Colorado Plateau on your face, Tempest," he kidded me. "Better make sure your words are as tough as your skin." I have not forgotten that. His words, tough as skin, are loyal to the earth, the earth that bore us and sustains us, the only home we shall ever know.

The rest of the day was spent sitting in pools, climbing in and out of alcoves, simply walking across desert meadows of prickly pears, globe mallows and cow pies. The same cow pies that fueled the *Moab Times Independent* with letters to the editors after his call for "no more cows, period!"

Abbey's humor solicited mine. We told stories. We walked in silence, just walked sharing the small wonders of the day in gentle conversation, in spirited debate. His gifts of listening, of asking the poignant questions, the barbs, the generosities ... this strong, tall desert of a man, both shy and fierce, reflective and combative, in love with his public and in revolt against them. This human being of complex paradox and passion who lured us out of complacency again and again. I hear his voice:

Delicate arch, a fragile ring of stone. If it holds any signifi-
cance, it lay in the power of the odd and unexpected to startle
the senses and surprise the mind out of their ruts of habit, to
compel us into a reawakened sense of the wonderful.

Ed could have been talking about himself. With Abbey,
anything was possible, hence his seduction. His broad smile,
his big, old hands, his unforgettable voice and cadence—that
was the last time I walked with him. The postcards kept coming, like a blizzard, like migrating birds, like shooting stars,
keeping in touch.

Last week, I went back through Millcreek Canyon, re-
traced our steps through slickrock, recalled the potholes that
brought us to our knees, the light dancing on redrock walls,
the soft sand, that beloved pink sand under boot, and the turkey vultures that always seemed to circle him with fondness,
with preference—who could blame them for their posses-
sive eye?

Things are different now. That's why we're here. Change
is growth, growth is life, and life is death. We are here to
honor Ed, to honor Clarke, Becky and Ben, Suzy, Aaron and
Josh, the Cartwrights, Howard and Nancy Abbey; to acknowledge family, tribe, and clan. And it has everything to
do with love: loving each other, loving the land. This is a re-
dedication of purpose and place.

The canyons of southern Utah are giving birth to the Coyote
Clan—hundreds, maybe even thousands of individuals who
are quietly subversive on behalf of the land. And they are in-
filtrating our neighborhoods in the most respectable ways,
with their long, bushy tails tucked discreetly inside their
pants or beneath their skirts.

Members of the Clan are not easily identified, but there

are clues. You can see it in their eyes. They are joyful and they are fierce. They can cry louder and laugh harder than anyone on the planet. And they have enormous range.

The Coyote Clan is a raucous bunch: they have drunk from desert potholes and belched forth toads. They tell stories with such virtuosity that you'll swear you have been in the presence of preachers.

The Coyote Clan is also serene. They can float on their backs down the length of any river or lose entire afternoons in the contemplation of stone.

Members of the Clan court risk and will dance on slick-rock as flash floods erode the ground beneath their feet. It doesn't matter. They understand the earth re-creates itself day after day. . . .

One last promise, Ed: we shall go forth with a vengeance.

A full moon is rising. Howl and wait for his echo. Abbey's voice. I hear it. "Feet on earth, knock on wood, touch stone, good luck to all."

And may I add, keep in touch—with Ed, with each other, and with the earth.

Love always, the Earth.

The Burial of Edward Abbey

While he lived, Ed Abbey attracted all manner of tall tales and near-legends, few of them true, many of them stories he enjoyed telling on himself. In death, Abbey continues to attract his share of apocrypha, often from the unlikeliest of sources: New York writers, passing acquaintances, performance artists—and even Parisian novelists.

In La Pierre et la saguaro *(The Stone and the Saguaro), published in Paris by Éditions Grasset & Fasquelle in 1990, Yves Berger recounts his supposed travels throughout the American West. The closing chapter of his best-selling book describes Abbey's burial, the details of which are fine fictions: an actual eyewitness tells us that no French-speaking person came within two hundred miles of the interment.*

But, as Ed Abbey would doubtless say, we should not let the facts get in the way of a good story.

There aren't many humans in this book. Doubtless because in the American Southwest I love only stones, saguaros, dead Indians. (Georgia O'Keeffe, too, had I been able to know her alive.) To these I add, but then you already know it: the sky, the rain, the brush, the stars, Santa Fe, the roadrunner . . . anything that smacks of the celestial, the sidereal, the ligneous, the mineral, the animal. There aren't any humans at all throughout *The Stone and the Saguaro*, in which for a long time I have thought of situating Edward Abbey.

By way of introduction, a man. No one knows him in France—not a bit of his thought or his style, because he has not been translated. His work? *Desert Solitaire*, his masterpiece, with eighteen printings in paperback, millions of copies. *Desert Solitaire* is an essay on the wonders of the Southwest by a man who, in order to get to know its nature and landscape as well as he could, became a ranger, a guard—or, better, guardian—of its waters and forests. You know what "waters and forests" means in the American Southwest. Something like the world itself. Edward Abbey, guardian of the world. Where? At Arches National Park, near the little town of Moab, in southeastern Utah. An emblematic place, brother or sister of the Grand Canyon, Bryce Canyon, Monument Valley. . . . He is also a novelist: *Black Sun* and, above all, *The Brave Cowboy*, a title there's no need to translate into French; from that book David Miller made the film *Lonely Are the Brave* in 1962, with the unsurpassable Kirk Douglas. A great Western.

With the stone and the saguaro, Edward Abbey was the third reason for my journey to the Southwest. We had exchanged letters and had agreed that I would call on my arrival at Los Angeles so that we could arrange to meet in Tucson, his hometown in the desert, right next door to the saguaros. I had taken a picture of him with my inner mind, starting from the clichés that represent such a man, and I carried the picture deep within me: large, strapping, with a big face and shaggy beard. Unkempt, like all Americans.

As soon as I landed in Los Angeles and checked into a hotel I called. He had died the day before.

Since the funeral was tentatively planned for two days hence, I scrapped my previous travel arrangements and hur-

ried to Tucson without delay. One of his friends awaited me
at his house and suggested that we go see Edward (Ed, as I
had never called him) at the mortuary. I refused. I had missed
him alive, and I didn't want to see a corpse. At least I thought
so then. My interlocutor, a very affable man, spent two hours
evoking the memory of the man whom I loved from afar and
whom, because of death, I would never befriend. Nevertheless, I felt terrible. . . . When I got up to take my leave I asked
once more where and when the funeral would take place, and
to my growing astonishment I could get no response until at
last my host decided to tell me: Edward would be buried in
the desert, which was against the law, the next morning before sunrise. Return here at three in the morning, here at
the home of Edward Abbey, where his body had been taken
earlier that evening.

Edward Abbey buried in the desert! His desert. His world.
I was convinced that somehow in his new abode he had
warned his followers that I would become one of them, a
neophyte.

At three o'clock sharp, dressed in warm garments that
someone had thought to lend me, I knocked at the door.
There stood the man who that evening had welcomed me
and kept me company. And a young woman with a tan so
deep and natural that I thought she must have been born
with it, then two Indians—a Navajo and a Hopi. Indians as
they have become: large, unsteady, already started on the
bourbon and beer. As soon as I had arrived and introductions
had been made, the whole group moved as one to a side room
where, awkward, I hesitated to follow. They quickly returned: the Navajo in the lead, the Hopi behind, they carried
Edward, strapped to a litter, dressed in thick clothes as if for
a polar expedition. They had not covered his suffering head,

and I looked in spite of myself: beautiful, proud, already far away.

A little truck called a "pickup," the horse of today's Indians, awaited us at the door. Someone put Ed on the bed, another covered him up, a third took the route to Sonora. The cab could hold only two people, making it necessary to climb in back, as I proceeded to do until the courteous company insisted that because I was a foreigner I should ride with the driver. I got the better end of the deal: on the bed, under a tarp, I again found the Hopi, the Navajo, and two whites, one of whom was my interlocutor of the evening before.

The truck felt like it was riding on rails, tough and flexible, through Tucson, sometimes in pitch black and sometimes bathed in light. We agreed on a signal: the young woman would smack the back of the cab twice, hard, to warn us if the police crossed our path. No problem.

We talked in the agonizing cold of night. I learned, or learned again, that Ed was sixty-two years old, that he had come down from the Appalachians at the age of seventeen and had never since left the West (or the Southwest). He loved it passionately. No one more than him, among them, had spent more nights under the beautiful stars.

The young woman was the last of the five women he had married and with whom he had fathered five children.

I sensed, at one point, that we were leaving the road. Doubtless we were on a dirt trail. The truck had to slow down. We climbed, descended. We teetered to the right, the left, ahead, behind. The vehicle jolted for a long time like that until at last it stopped.

Someone helped me out of the truck. It was exactly five o'clock. The first rays of dawn, still hidden, did nothing more than dissolve a few shadows, but it made me aware that we were now on an immense flat desert plain. I spotted mountains and mesas around us and afar.

Desert solitaire.

I took a few steps, which put me right in front of the truck, where I saw two other men who had surely dug the pit that now opened before us, deep, dark, the excavated sand piled up in a great heap next to another large pile of stones.

I instinctively raised my eyes and saw—it warmed my heart in the piercing cold—the great crescent of the moon hanging in the sky, rimmed by stars that crowded in on themselves so that the whole sky seemed like one big star that had burst into millions of pieces of shining white confetti. I lowered my eyes at the moment the two white men lowered Edward into the ground. The young woman sobbed.

I caught a glimpse of the Navajo, who carried what seemed to me to be a jar. It was. Everyone's eyes fixed on him. He opened the jar, dipped his hands into it, pulled them out dripping and passed them over Edward Abbey's darkening face. I learned later that Edward had asked that this Apache rite be performed there, as it had been for Cochise a hundred years earlier.

The Hopi had climbed back into the cab. At one point he flashed the headlights and in the sudden light he surprised two coyotes who had been sneaking up silently in the night, troubled by the lonely whispers of these light-emitting creatures. They fled, howling a sharp howl that seemed to detach itself from the very deepest part of their voices. Edward had revealed to me, in one of his letters of the year before, that to break the solitude of his firewatch in the Grand Canyon he had learned to imitate (to play?) the staccato cries of the coyote on his flute. Descending into the grave, the Hopi took Edward from the hands of the whites and the Navajo.

I kept back a little, like someone not truly, ever, at all part of the desert.

The Hopi climbed back out. We waited a good while, sheepish, to look at Edward stretched out at the bottom of the pit, while the sun rose. Until one of the white men gathered a handful of earth and motioned to the woman to do the same. She threw the desert sand into the grave and, after her, everyone else did the same.

We hadn't said a single word since we arrived, and I jumped when I heard someone say, "It's time."

The Navajo, the Hopi, and one of the whites took up shovels and in no time at all the earth covered the hole, and then the rocks on top of dirt. The place looked as though it had not been disturbed.

The three men straightened up, and we all looked at one another, and I felt that we had come to achieve something great and beautiful and noble, the meaning of which I only half understood.

For the first time, I had a good view of the area. Full of ocotillos, cactus everywhere, lining the crags, of red flat earth that went on and on, to die at the foot of the far-distant mesas, as far as the eye could see. Without looking for him, my steps took me to the proud Hopi, who knelt staring at the sand. He thought that I was interested in the tracks there, and he pointed them out to me one by one, his hand sweeping over the earth: the California hare, the kit fox, the cottontail (he could tell its tracks from those of the hare and the common rabbit!), the diamondback rattlesnake, the kangaroo rat, a lizard that I imagined must have looked prehistoric by the way it moved, and, for my pleasure, the roadrunner. Edward would not be alone.

I heaved myself into the back of the truck, the driver

started it up, and to celebrate or curse our departure the coyotes let out various howls, then a long moan that covered up the roar of the motor, making my already heavy heart heavier, suddenly seized by anguish. The sun, down at the far east of the sky, was an enormous incandescent ball gorged with blood, so huge and at that moment so immobile that it threatened to roll over or fall down, and I knew that if either of these eventualities came about the world would burn to death among these bursting rocks, these consumed saguaros. I had put myself in the bed so that I could see up to the last moment Edward's tomb, that hole in the desert of stone and saguaro, and at the moment I lost sight of it I heard Kathleen Lloyd ask Jack Nicholson in *The Missouri Breaks*, "Why don't we just take a walk," adding, "and we'll just talk about the Wild West and how to get the hell out of it," and I knew that, like Edward Abbey, I would never leave it until I died.

Translated by Gregory McNamee

DAVID PETERSEN

Where Phantoms Come to Brood and Mourn

There is a valley in the West where phantoms come to brood and mourn, pale phantoms dying of nostalgia and bitterness. You can hear them, shivering, chattering, among the leaves of the old dry mortal cottonwoods down by the river—whispering and moaning and hissing with the wind . . . whining their past away with the wild dove and the mockingbird—and you may see one, touch one, in the silences and space and mute terror of the desert.   Edward Abbey

It is March 14, 1992, the third anniversary of Edward Abbey's premature death. He was a writer, of course, a damned good one, and the godfather of so-called radical environmentalism. But this isn't about either of those things.

I am sitting in the desert sand beside Abbey's hidden grave, talking and joking and weeping with him, and smoking a cheap cigar—not the kind he preferred, but the kind he smoked a lot of; even for the "Thoreau of the American West" (actually, he was better than that), life was often a compromise. It has been a pilgrimage, or as close to one as I'll likely ever come, this visit to the last refuge of the man

I respected and loved more than any other. And befitting a true pilgrimage, the way here has not been entirely easy.

After a tiring road trip, my guide and I veer off the blacktop back-road. I lock in my old truck's four-by-four hubs and we go grinding down a sandy desert two-track. A long time later, we reach the end of the jeep trail, where we will make camp. The rest of the way will be afoot.

As I swig water and otherwise prepare for a desert hike, my guide kneels and scratches a map in the sun-warmed sand, points westward, speaks a few soft words. From here, by choice, I am on my own. It's at least an hour's fast hike over prickly, unfamiliar terrain, she says. With little more than two hours of daylight left, I step out briskly.

I must be vague in this narrative. The shrine I am seeking is on public land and no burial permit was applied for; nor, most likely, would one have been granted. Ed needs his privacy. I am sworn, therefore, to a pact of secrecy.

And it's really best this way. By being nowhere in particular, Edward Abbey, whose writing and personal example has meant so much to so many, is now everywhere in spirit, happily haunting every slickrock promontory, every slot canyon, every cedar-scented mesa, every hidden valley, every wild place remaining in the American Southwest. If you know about Abbey, if you've read *Desert Solitaire*, *The Monkey Wrench Gang*, *The Fool's Progress*, *Confessions of a Barbarian* or any other of Ed's two dozen books, then you know the sort of place I'm so carefully not describing here. Abbey Country.

I stride on, dividing my attention between the ground approaching my boots and the rocky, ragged western horizon. It is warm but not hot; maybe eighty in the sun. Perfect.

Half an hour out, a shadow like a B-52 slips across the ground ahead of me, crossing from right to left. I stop and look up. Between me and a blinding sun, a huge dark form glides in easy spirals on a thermal whirlpool. I look down for a moment, then squint my eyes and glance again at the indistinct, haloed silhouette. An eagle, possibly. Too big for hawk, raven or falcon. Nor is it likely a turkey buzzard; the wings lack sufficient dihedral, the tail is too broadly fanned. Too bad. How appropriate it would be just now if that *were* a scuzzy old vulture circling up there—Abbey's afterlife alter ego.

"Given a choice," he wrote in "Watching the Birds," "I plan to be a long-winged fantailed bird next time around. Which one? Vulture, eagle, hawk, falcon, crane, heron, wood ibis? Well, I believe I was a wood ibis once, back in the good old days of the Pleistocene epoch. And from what I already know of passion, violence, the intensity of the blood, I think I'll pass on eagle, hawk or falcon this time. For a lifetime or two, or maybe three, I think I'll settle for the sedate career, serene and soaring, of the humble turkey buzzard. . . . And contemplate this world we love from a silent and considerable height."

Alas, the long-winged fan-tailed bird up there contemplating this particular bit of the world from a silent and considerable height is no vulture. And just as well. Like Ed himself acknowledged toward the end of his avian musings, "As appealing as I find the idea of reincarnation, I must confess that it has a flaw: to wit, there is not a shred of evidence suggesting it might be true."

Anyhow, my big bird, of whatever feather, is deserting me, fading fast into the glaring west, chasing the sun down the afternoon sky.

And I had best get back to my own chase. My feet pick up the pace until the rough-and-tumble terrain is flowing past in a soft blur. Flat to gently rolling, this is hiking heaven compared to the uphill-both-ways San Juan Mountains of southwest Colorado, my home stamping grounds. Even so, hiking here is complicated by a litter of sharp-edged rocks and a plague of cacti and other prickly desert vegetation, necessitating constant vigilance and frequent dodging, providing plenty of opportunity to stub a toe, twist an ankle, stumble and fall, maybe trod upon an indolent rattler. Hiking out across here with just a light pack, as I am now, is one thing, but toting a six-foot-three, 180-pound man any distance over this natural obstacle course would be something else entirely.

But a fistful of good and loyal friends did exactly that, honoring Ed's wishes to be "transported in the bed of a pickup truck and buried as soon as possible after death. No undertakers wanted, no embalming (for godsake!), no coffin. Just an old sleeping bag. . . . I want my body to help fertilize the growth of a cactus, or cliffrose, or sagebrush, or tree."

While he was about it, Ed had a little fun arranging his own wake, calling for bagpipes, a bonfire, "a flood of beer and booze! Lots of singing, dancing, talking, hollering, laughing and love-making. No formal speeches desired, though if someone feels the urge, the deceased will not interfere."

Ed got all of that and more at what was surely the biggest party Saguaro National Monument has ever hosted. I spent most of the day prostrate in the stingy shade of a paloverde tree—stoned in the morning, drunk in the afternoon—trying my best, like the other hundred or so mourners there, to smile and laugh and deny the tragedy that had brought us together. No matter that Ed had assured us that "it is not death or dying which is tragic, but rather to have existed without fully participating in life—that is the deepest personal tragedy."

Edward Abbey suffered his share of life's tragedies. But lack of active participation was not among them. He had fun.

I'm occasionally asked what the "real" Edward Abbey was like: Did the laughing farting animate *man* bear any resemblance to "Cactus Ed," the eloquently gruff, gloriously ornery literary persona of his autobiographical prose?

I'd say the two were essentially identical. Not even Abbey the writer could invent a character as colorful and complex as Abbey the man. The Edward Abbey I knew was joyful and easygoing most of the time but fierce in argument, alternately sensitive and crass as dictated by company and circumstance, the perfect gentleman if he thought you deserved it, a loving husband and father, a loyal and generous friend, impossible to pigeonhole.

Of course, I came into the picture rather late, and there had been an Edward Abbey I did not know—the young restless quixotic version. That Abbey, along the way to becoming the Ed I knew, had experienced his share of troubles, most of them of the flirty-skirty variety. "How can I be true to just one woman," he would feign to ponder, grinning slyly, "without being untrue to all the rest?"

Good question. Edward Abbey was no saint, thank God.

Lost in these musings, time and distance pass quickly and after about an hour of speed-hiking I am standing atop the promontory near where I've been told Ed is holed up these days, relaxing in his favorite sleeping bag. I survey the scene—a large, flat-topped expanse of rock, sand, cactus—then walk to a place that looks more or less right. And there I find . . . rock, sand, cactus. The perfection of nothingness.

Pure hunch having failed me, I decide to try a pinch of method, and spend the next several minutes pacing back and forth across the promontory in something loosely approximating a grid search. *Nada.*

Time grows short. Fifteen minutes more and I'll be wandering around out here like Moses when the lights went off. Just me and the bats, the owls and somewhere . . .

I'm admiring a sunset as beautiful and improbable as life itself, pondering where to search next, darkness creeping over the land and shadowing my hopes, when I hear the lonesome cooing of a male mourning dove. The melancholy music rises from somewhere beyond the promontory's rim, down a slope that drops off toward a desert valley spreading south and west beyond sight—broad, barren, eerie as hell beneath the deep-purple twilight. No roads, no buildings, no lights down there. Only a pure, clean, peaceful emptiness—the way I imagine death.

Without questioning the impulse, I go skidding and sliding down the slope, homing on the calling dove. And why not? At this point, one direction seems as good as another, and the valley view from down there should be superb. As I draw noisily near, the mourner falls silent and wings away, a ghostly gray shadow dissolving into the gloaming.

Fighting back creeping despair, determined to search through the night if necessary—I have water, fruit, matches, compass, a windbreaker and flashlight in my pack, and the weather is sublime—I turn and start back up the slope, bumbling blindly through the dying minutes of the day . . . and bumble hard into a low-lying cactus, kicking a trident of nettlesome spines through the thin nylon of my boot top and deep into my left foot.

After breaking off all three brittle shafts in a clumsy, half-panicked attempt to quickly rid myself of their searing pain, I am forced to sit down and unlace and delicately remove the boot, peel back the sock and use the little folding pliers I carry in a belt pouch to extract the hot-barbed tips. Somewhere off in the shadows, a coyote laughs at my predicament.

Only now—throbbing with self-inflicted pain, one shoe off and one shoe on like some dippy nursery rhyme character, mumbling disparagements at myself for not paying more attention to where my feet were landing, cursing the coyote for his arrogant and insensitive scorn—only now do I look up and see, no more than six feet from my sunburned nose, a native rock the size and shape of a badger and bearing a neatly chiseled inscription, which I squint to read in the failing light:

EDWARD PAUL ABBEY

1927–1989

NO COMMENT

So and at last it has come to pass that I am sitting here in the desert sand beside an old friend's hidden grave, talking and joking and weeping with him, and smoking a cheap cigar. What's left of it.

"No Comment" was Ed's reply when asked by a friend if he had any last words for posterity. A joker to the end, that Abbey.

Life can be strange. I like to think of myself as a down-to-earth man. Mysticism is not my magic. Yet, here I sit in a remote sundown desert, alone but not entirely, dumbfounded by the double coincidence of dove call and cactus spine that would seem to have pointed me here—which *did* point me here—to this place I've wanted and needed for so long to be. And the timing of the coyote's laugh. It would be easy, almost tempting, to *not* dismiss it all as mere coincidence, given the circumstances.

"Do you believe in ghosts?" Ed once asked himself in his journals, answering, "Those that haunt the human soul, yes." In that respect, at least, I am truly haunted. Beyond that, it's hard to know *what* to think just now.

But I do know what Ed would think, what he'd say about the eerie coincidence of events and this superstitious line of thought (I almost said, "were he here"). He'd grin that wicked lupine grin of his, shrug, and offer, "Who knows? Who cares? And what difference does it make anyhow?"

Good questions.

I mouth the stump of my deceased cigar, stare at the modest headstone—perfect—and fall again to musing, casting back across the precious little time I was privileged to spend with Edward Paul Abbey, the man whose fellow writers (he had no peers) have called "brash, irresponsibly satiric, happily excessive . . . a full-blooded man . . . a man 'still with the bark on' . . . man of character and courage . . . the original fly in the ointment . . . a gadfly with a stinger like a scorpion . . . a rebel and an eloquent loner . . . a national treasure" . . . and occasionally, by those lacking the open-minded intelligence to stay with him, things far less generous.

The last time I saw Edward Abbey was just after Thanksgiving, 1988. He, his young wife Clarke and their lap-sized children Rebecca and Benjamin had sardined themselves into the cab of Ed's old pickup truck and driven the five hundred miles from Tucson up to my hometown of Durango in southwestern Colorado.

They had come for a book signing at Maria's, an elegant (Ed's term) little Southwest-flavored bookshop owned by Dusty Teal, an old river-ratting pal of Ed's. It was a favor typical of Abbey's generosity to friends, and the last stop, an addendum actually, to a murderous four-week, coast-to-coast tour for *The Fool's Progress*. Ed was frankly relieved to have that particular job of work behind him, swearing it was "absolutely the *last* time" he'd ever tour. (Suggesting there more than I could know.)

Ed seemed to enjoy himself immensely on that final visit, elated to be back in the rural Southwest, back home. Cheery and chipper, him.

For an instance: At a restaurant one evening, Ed complained to our waiter about the size of his dinner napkin, pretending outrage, calling it "A damn postage stamp!" The waiter was game, taking away the offending napkin and returning momentarily with a checkered tablecloth. Not to be one-upped, Ed accepted the sail-sized replacement with a serious, deep-voiced "Now *that's* more like it." Unfurling the prize, he tucked a fat corner into his collar and resumed his meal. Only after the waiter had left did he break into a huge, triumphant grin.

The next day, we drove up onto a piñon-juniper mesa a few miles above town and hiked for an hour into a biting late-November wind, walking and talking the cold away. Despite the unfriendly weather, Ed had insisted on a hike.

Abbey was a walker, doing a mile or two most every morning, again in the cool of evening, and finding the time for frequent days-long backpack treks. Once, pushing sixty, equipped with an old Kelty pack, aspirin and Demerol, he hiked 115 miles in six days, alone, across perhaps the truest desert wilderness North America has left. Each night's hike (he rested through the blistering middays) was a life-or-death race to reach another water source before the morning sun attacked him. (Ed would later suggest that the rivers of highly alkaline desert water he'd drunk in his long career of desert ratting might have contributed to the esophageal bleeding that was slowly killing him.)

Though we always walked when we got together—up and down the desert wash that meanders close behind *chez* Abbey on the west edge of Tucson, among the sandstone hobgoblins of southeast Utah, amongst the cool aspen forests surrounding my mountain cabin—I'd never gotten to join Ed on a *real* hike. During that last little stroll together above Durango, we laid plans to remedy that. There was a place, he told me, a magical desert valley. We'd go there soon . . . Ed, our good friend Jack Loeffler and I would rendezvous in March for a week of wilderness camping and hiking and companionable bull-shooting. Perfect.

At visit's end, Ed handed me a copy of *The Fool's Progress*, held open to an inscription scrawled large on the title page: "For my good friend Dave Petersen and his great wife Caroline—companions on this fool's journey out of the dark, through the light, into the unknown."

I knew that Ed had been sick, off and on, for quite some time, but I was unaware of just how *very* sick. I had no idea, certainly, that he was dying, nor did many others; I guess he didn't want to burden anyone unnecessarily. (Now, how I wish he'd burdened me.) But even in my ignorance, that haunting *Fool's Progress* inscription foreshadowed the dark side. Standing there with that huge heavy book in my hand, I recalled . . .

- My first nervous meeting with Edward Abbey, famous writer and (I'd been warned) curmudgeon extraordinaire. I had traveled to Tucson to conduct a magazine interview—a meeting it had taken me weeks of letter-writing and uneasy telephone conversations to win. We met on the patio at the venerable and elegant (Ed's term) Arizona Inn and talked through a lovely Sonoran January day, nursing Coronas to ease the tension between strangers. It worked. ("Beer for breakfast," Ed observed, loosening up, "is one of the good things in life.") Our conversation ranged late into the night and was the longest and most detailed interview Ed would ever give. It was also the beginning of a friendship destined to die even as it flowered.

- The time I asked Ed to write an essay for a magazine I was helping to launch—it would impress my employer and gain the fledgling publication instant attention—and Ed politely, reluctantly declining, explaining that he was already swamped with writing commitments. Then, a week or so later, "River Solitaire" arrived, accompanied by a note saying "I found this story in my journals and typed it up. It's fairly loose writing, but it's yours if you want it." Loose writing it certainly was not, and I knew that Ed had taken time he didn't have in order to help a friend.
- That awkward time Ed spontaneously offered to loan me a thousand dollars, no conditions, when I carelessly grumbled that times were a little hard.
- His generous mentorship, repeatedly offering to sponsor me, and other struggling writer-friends, with his agent and publishers.
- And, most vividly, I recalled the experience that had introduced me to Cactus Ed—my first reading of *Desert Solitaire*. It was that book, more than any other stimulus, that opened my sleepy eyes to the heartbreaking beauty of the natural world, to the bittersweet mystery of life on this miraculous earth, our one true home. "The only home," Ed had written, "we will ever know." It is not hyperbole to say that *Desert Solitaire* changed my life.

We shook hands, exchanged *abrazos*, said our so-longs— "*Adios, amigo*. See you in March for that camping trip." Then Ed bent into the truck alongside his family—and was gone.

On March 4, the day before I was to leave for our desert rendezvous, complications at home forced me to phone

Ed and beg off. Graciously, he concurred with my excuses. "Don't worry about it," he said. "There'll always be another day."

Ten days later, Ed Abbey was dead. He was only sixty-two.

Thinking back on that last phone conversation now, Ed was right—there *would* be another day, and this is it.

I inhale deep the light desert air, wondering at the mysterious spicy fragrances rising from the blackness of the valley below—the selfsame valley, ironically, that Ed had wanted to share with me three years ago. It is a place, I am learning, where phantoms come to brood and mourn.

If you go there you must hear them . . . where the air is cool and sweet with the odor of juniper and lightning, where the mockingbird and the canyon wren and the mourning dove join with the phantoms in their useless keening.

Abbey country.

I squat beside the crude headstone and say to Ed the things I've come all the long way here to say, then lace boot loosely over injured foot, pull on my pack, stand and tip my cap to this good, wise man I was so very fortunate to have known. As a parting gesture—there's nobody here to call me maudlin—I place a Marsh Wheeling, the cigar Ed most preferred but rarely indulged in, on the sand in front of his headstone. Then I turn and limp out into the night, resuming my own fool's journey through the dark, into the unknown.

Saying Adios to Ed

Wednesday, the twenty-second of March, 1989, began as a fine hot morning in the desert surrounding Tucson, Arizona. To the west of the city, in the most distant picnic ground of Saguaro National Monument, several dozen women, men, and children gathered to say farewell to their dear friend Ed Abbey, who had died nine days earlier.

The farewell—a celebration much more than a funeral— was, we learned, the product of Ed's careful orchestration. (I saw notes for the event, in his hand.) It began with the consumption of a great many glasses of good champagne, while a bagpiper played Scottish tunes—"Amazing Grace," "The Bonnie Lassie," "Loch Lomond." At about eleven o'clock, Robert Houston read from his essay "Down the River with Edward Abbey." He was followed by Leslie Marmon Silko, who read movingly from *Desert Solitaire*, crying at the end. Ed's daughter Susie, a student at Sarah Lawrence College, then read his essay "Two Cheers for Anarchy," eliciting just that from the crowd. Immediately afterward, from a nearby thicket of saguaro, the photographer Jack Dykinga played taps on a bugle, bringing the crowd to open and unashamed tears.

The drinking continued, with no one seeming the worse for it. Plates of tortillas and tamales, a "slow elk" stew made from a cow that had unfortunately trodden on our public lands, salads, baguettes, rounds of smoked cheeses, vegetables, and cold meats were produced. David Laird, then librarian of the University of Arizona, handed around a copy of the twentieth anniversary edition of *Desert Solitaire* for all there to sign. This, he said, would be entered into the Abbey archive in Special Collections.

At about three in the afternoon, the once seemingly endless supply of alcohol threatened to run out, and Dave Foreman set about collecting money for a beer run, hat in hand. Thirty seconds later, he had two hundred dollars. Volunteers from the Earth First! contingent loaded into a Volkswagen, impossibly small, and trundled up the mountain road to Tucson, returning with cases of Mexican beer and quarts of tequila, scotch, and vodka. In the interim, John Davis produced a tape of Ed's last reading, a hilarious and moving recitation from *Hayduke Lives!;* Ed's adult sons Josh, an actor, and Aaron, a writer and biology student, read eulogies; Bob Greenspan, an itinerant guitarist, set up shop, using a gasoline-powered generator for his amplifier and launching into several rowdy anthems, including a favorite Abbey tune, "Big Tits, Braces and Zits." Doug Peacock fired a pistol into the air, park rangers milled about smiling, and a child announced that he had seen two people making love in a dry wash nearby.

It was an equally fine morning two months later, when a much larger audience, numbering about six hundred by most estimates, gathered on the edge of Arches National Monument to say their farewells. Watching that group and listening to the speakers who had come forward to offer their remarks on Ed's passing—among them Ken "Seldom Seen" Sleight, C. L. Rawlins, John DePuy, Wendell Berry, Barry Lopez, Terry Tempest Williams, and Ann Zwinger—I was struck by just how many people Edward Abbey knew and cared for in life, how many people looked to him for inspiration and guidance, and how he gave freely of himself while still attending to all the many things a working writer must. I was struck, too, at the square dance that followed out at Ken Sleight's Pack Creek Ranch, there on a shoulder of the holy mountain Tukuhnikivats, by the very Americanness of Ed Abbey's life, his resisting much and obeying little, and the farewell itself. Jim Bishop captures something of that spirit in his homage to Abbey, *Epitaph for a Desert Anarchist*; so do the speakers and writers who follow.

Doug Peacock's and Dave Foreman's speeches from that event were first transcribed and published, in somewhat different form, in the *Journal of Energy, Natural Resources and Environmental Law* Vol. 11, No. 1 (1990). Charles Bowden's essay first appeared in the *Arizona Daily Star* on March 18, 1989; the other texts come from a special supplement to the *Tucson Weekly*, published on April 5, 1989.

Gregory McNamee

Gary Paul Nabhan

Ed Abbey is one whom I will remember for the sometimes brilliant, sometimes humorous images he gave us, not for his polemics or his personal style. Long after I have forgotten what his philosophy was on wilderness without handrails, women without mates, Mexican immigrants, anarchy, the right to bear arms, and the right to arm bears, I will remember the images he branded into our brain cells. The brave cowboy escaping, only to be run down by a trucker. The fire burning on the mountain and in a nonconformist's eyes. Lost on a solo hike below Supai. Picking wildflowers of pas-

tel Kleenex along the roadside of a national park. Throwing
beer cans out along the roadside of a Mexican highway to dis-
courage Gringo tourism. Shooting a refrigerator dead.
Twice.

Like that other misanthropic humanitarian I love—Robinson Jeffers—Abbey had a well-worn redundancy regarding
the philosophical issues he addressed. This bored the tears
out of some readers and provided a steady touchstone for
others. He, like Jeffers in his own time, was noticeably out of
step with the policies, the pretensions and devices of liberal
writers from the East and West coasts. In the end, who cares?
He will make compost just as fine as those with whom he
argued.

Unlike Jeffers, however, Abbey enriched us with his humor. If his words can do anything, they can make us laugh at
the human condition. The way a captionless *Far Side* cartoon
can. The way Ry Cooder's rasty version of the song "I Got
Mine" can.

After a couple years of being ticked off at Abbey's verbal
wars with Murray Bookchin, Gretel Ehrlich and others—
because I cared more for his creative fiction than for his letters to the editor and enemies—I worked one day in the desert listening to tapes of his readings. By the end of the day
my face hurt from laughing and smiling too much. He had
brought a slapstick hilarity to a genre too serious about itself—environmental writing. Not nature writing, mind
you. Something larger than that. He could describe the tension in a redneck bar in an Arizona mining town as well as
he could describe the Maze. (The main difference between
the two environments is that he got thrown out of the former
more frequently.)

For me, that humor is what sets Abbey apart from
the other great desert writers: Joseph Wood Krutch, Ann
Woodin, Ann Zwinger, Barry Lopez, and Charles Bowden.

His landmark contribution is in being the first literary naturalist to make us laugh, to keep us from crying about the state of the earth. Abbey had a greater capacity for poking fun at our feeble ways, for juxtaposing the wimpiness of our species with the grandeur of our settings. He chortled at being the best-selling author in Moab and Mexican Hat, for he knew that the canyons around there could elicit more ecstasy than anything found in those towns.

Somewhere in those canyons perhaps his voice is still echoing, "Joy, sheepmates, Joy! Joy! Joy!"

Ann Zwinger

Ed and I were on a river trip down Lodore Canyon one bloody cold October. One of the three rafts wrapped around a big rock in the middle of the river, spewing out all the gear and popping a strap on my wet bag. Hypothermia dictated that everything be dry before nightfall. Ed stood for an hour like a mooring post, patiently holding my lumpy, luffing dirigible of a sleeping bag up to the wind to dry. In subsequent years he prevented in all of us who read him mental hypothermia, was generous with praise, and always faced up to the wind.

Peter Warshall

I knew Ed mostly as a writer. I lived in the home in which he wrote *Desert Solitaire*. We never spent time together in the desert scrub—a place we're both more at home. We both loved Van Dyke's *The Desert*. We talked awkwardly—mostly about other writers. We talked about "naturalist writers," which were not his bag. He preferred the ironic imagination to taxonomic accuracy, the telling of the tale to foodweb complexity. In discussing the spadefoot toad, he asked: Why do they sing? Has joy any survival value in the operation of evolution? "I suspect it does," he wrote in *Desert Solitaire*. "I suspect that the morose and fearful are doomed to quick extinction. Where there is no joy there can be no courage; and without courage all other virtues are useless." As the naturalist, I had argued that the spadefoot's courage came from its poison, from its skin. Behind an armor of warts, the spadefoot can fearlessly bleat love songs. Its "medicine" is stronger than a coyote's stomach. This was our kind of talk— in fits and starts and spaced encounters.

Ed died as I am recovering from near death—a triple flip of a Land Rover in Botswana. I wanted to keep these events separate. But, in the heart, they mix. What is it that creates death or lets the body temporarily hightail death pursuit? My friends speculate about the flow of his blood going astray—about dams blocking the free flow of rivers, about dams in the body, about the life-blood of the Earth body becoming channeled, and the internal bleeding of the Earth body within its skin of sky. In death or near death, in confronting it, you can't untangle your own blood from the planet's waters, our flesh from the planet's earth; the plumbing doesn't stop at the human skin. That's what Ed wanted his readers to know. In both life and death.

The animal that I saw near death was the mole excavating a braille geometry of underworld passages in absolute darkness. When Ed died, the packrat, the lovely, Mickey Mouse-eared deer rat popped up. Ed's totem, the bearer of many messages of his memory. We had talked of packrats. One packrat, in particular, who lives at the highest altitude in the southwest—near the peak of Mt. Graham and Emerald Peak. This heavenly packrat will have to move or die to make room for telescopes. That was Ed's final reading in Tucson. What's more important? This life on the planet or cold, black holes in another galaxy? The mystery of a high-altitude packrat or some melodramatic claim that hi-tech telescopes will lead to an increased understanding of man in the universe. Choose? As opposed to the philistines, he insisted that you can't always have both.

We had talked of post-Pleistocene packrats whose middens, concealed by piss and time, gave him a chuckle about who or what would last longer: the techno-monuments of career-panicked academics, knee-jerk engineers, dull bureaucrats, dulled developers and even duller politicos or the acquisitive packrat stashing, for posterity, a piece of broken mirror from a newfangled telescope. He enjoyed these kinds of thoughts.

An old friend and neighbor told me the news. I drove around Tucson, regaining confidence in motorized vehicles, mixing thoughts of walking, spadefoots, the solstitial moon, the hope of late rains, and the stench of desert rat death. The desert rat—the one I was thinking on—liked the rock house sunk into caliche and colluvial gravel. It had settled in between roof and ceiling, chewed the insulation off the swamp cooler ducts, carried mirrorlike pop tops, gum wrappers and spare change into its nest, cultured a midden-full of assassin bugs that invaded the living room, bit the shit out of my back, and sent me dancing down to St. Mary's Emergency for ephedrine shots and benadryl.

Starting from love, we set Havaharts. The Havaharts were robbed by packrat geniuses. Then, humongous snap traps. One dead, but the overhead pitter-patter had reproduced into swarming steps. We added spice to the bait: raisins to the peanut butter. But desert rats are no dummies. More assassin bugs emerged from the walls. We retreated to a mosquito net. Leaped paranoid, when reading on the couch. A neighbor said: Time for the Gopher-Go, the horrible-to-wildlife, never-use-in-lakes, strictly strychnine, all-machine-made poison.

You can't remove the dead, deep in the void between roof and ceiling. You can try snaking for them with an industrial vacuum hose, maybe even suck up an assassin bug, but it's best to just wait the three days, until the carcass dries, and contemplate the stench. What's the meaning of the desert rat stench? What drives a lover of desert rats to poison? Where did the negotiations between nature and culture collapse? Are we de-vo packrats, baiting ourselves with sweets? ultimately poisoning ourselves. How much of the thorny, hard-assed desert will we allow among the ranchettes?

Ed, the Southwest's great arid rodential philosopher, had no use for diplomacy. Ed hated it—the fetid odor and language of it. Over the past quarter century, human Desert Rats have covered their melancholia, their bitter angers in diplomatic sombreros. The human Desert Scalpers have sugar-coated their greed with bolo-tie diplomacy. California tried transforming diplomacy's stench into perfume—thank you, thank you for sharing your experience. But the Colorado's circulatory system has been blown. The river's blood covers the land of Abbey's novels. Pitted against imported, SoCal lust for land and money, diplomacy and Ed could find no safe home, no easy midden. Better to birdshoot sacred cows. Local sacred cows like Mo Udall and his deliberate diplomatic congressional destruction of the Sonoran desert. Better to stir up the citizenry—the contented cattleman, the baby boomer Mexican, the sober environmental lawyer who believes laws were meant for everyone.

His audience, his followers, frankly all of us, needed him. Earth First! increasingly became his material, his narrative voice and the recipient of some of his royalties. In urban apartments, broken adobes, and North Face tents, the rat-feet sing "No compromise in defense of Mother Earth" and "We live to fight another day." His brash voice cut through the foul breath of doublespeak. His novels slid down the slickrock to allegory. Not the dreadful serious, pious *Pilgrim's Progress*, but a slightly mean, all-too-accurate, fuck-here's-what-I-think allegory in *The Fool's Progress*. He exorcised bile by laughter. 'Midst 'whelming stench, his prose, the irritating pitter-patter of the desert rats. Please, sit down on this cactus, won't you?

Trail-clearers, hunters, firefighters, eco-radicals, animal lovers, river-runners, frustrated hikers, wildlife bureaucrats (with an Ed Abbey book in an ammo box, pack sack, or closed desk drawer) sniff with the Abbey outdoor nose. Ah, the stench of destruction in the chaparral.

Ed was no misanthrope. He just preferred outdoor employees trying to heal government's piecemeal whittling of wilderness and workers with both feet in awesome landscapes. A nature prejudice. He liked questionably illegal, mock heroic, theatrical, moral, seriously funny lessons and bleating confirmations from the spadefoots. As he wrote: "Do not burn yourself out. Be as I am—a reluctant enthusiast, a part-time crusader, a half-hearted fanatic. Save the other half of yourself for pleasure and adventure. It is not enough to fight for the West. It is even more important to enjoy it. While you can. While it's still there. So get out there and hunt and fish and mess around with your friends, explore the forests, encounter the griz, climb the mountains, run the rivers. Sit quietly for a while and contemplate the precious stillness, the loverly mysterious space."

John Nichols

Give the man his due, he kicked up a lot of good dust and raised a fine brand of hell. Wrote with a lyricism that sang, and an outrage that was full-bore, no-nonsense, straight as a desert highway headed south. His work is as exquisitely virulent as Jonathan Swift's, and at times just as funny. The man knew how to act like a fool, too, take a major-league pratfall, and outrage all his friends. He had ten times the number of enemies required to be considered an honorable man, but he just never chose to stop when he was ahead. He made us laugh, and he made us want to take up the cudgel and hit 'em where it hurts. Made us cry a lot, too, for what we used to be, for what we've done, for where we're headed now. Every time I open up my mouth to badger a group of folks, I find myself quoting his words: "Growth for the sake of growth is the ideology of the cancer cell." "Eat less beef." "A man by himself hasn't got a fucking chance." A caustic and gentle curmudgeon, a contrary hillbilly ecologist, this obdurate, frowning, portentous, laughing man knew how to sing in the rain, sidestep rattlesnakes gracefully, and make an eloquent case for the planet Earth. So: screw Star Wars, boys ... damn the roaring bulldozers, kids ... and round up all the coyotes, Man—let's howl up a storm of praise and indignation in honor of this cantankerous son of a bitch. And please, no 21-gun salute discharged uselessly at the stars, let's aim those bullets where they'll do the most good. And take off your John Deere cap, buddy, set down your beer can for a moment, and wipe that tear from your eye—

Ed Abbey's passing by.

Barbara Kingsolver

For years, Ed Abbey was a man I didn't want to know. We occasionally said hello in the post office, and that was enough. While I admired his ferocious reverence for the land, much of what he said about people sounded to me like bigotry; his proscriptions for Latin American refugees were frankly brutal, and on the subject of women he was given to remarks so anachronistically patronizing that they were either annoying or absurd.

When I learned last year that he and I would be meeting to co-judge the *Tucson Weekly*'s fiction contest, I was doubtful. I complained to a friend, "Me and Abbey at a restaurant, trying to agree on something? Sounds like a Blind Date from Hell."

It was nothing of the kind. Abbey was gracious, respectful to the point of deference, and wonderfully guileless. We had both had unlucrative careers as musicians, before becoming writers, and he reminisced about his beatnik days as a flute-player at an Albuquerque coffeehouse. (He was fired after some incensed townsfolk shot out the windows.) It dawned on me that the revolution of his youth was not the same one as mine. While Abbey was inspiring the ire of cowboys with his black turtleneck and beret, Gloria Steinem and Malcolm X were still awaiting conversion and I hadn't yet learned to walk. His language came out of a time I never knew. I decided to lighten up a little on Ed.

By the evening's end we had ascertained that we were neighbors and had children of the same age, and also that we had a lot of similar thoughts on writing. We exchanged phone numbers. As we were leaving, I asked him, "Do you just do the Old-Bastard image so people will leave you alone?" He gave me an absolutely radiant smile and said, "Yep."

I assumed I'd have all the time in the world to cultivate his acquaintance. I didn't, and I regret it.

Kevin Dahl

Ed Abbey once tried to steal my girlfriend.

Years later, the incident is my best Ed Abbey story. No one

cares to hear much about the cigar he gave me when a bunch of us committed civil disobedience against the cruise missile. Eyes glass over when I start telling how my first letter to Abbey, a request for his help, was returned with an outstanding letter in support of a wilderness area my group had proposed, along with a $100 contribution. Even the amazing coincidence of our chance meeting on an Alaskan ferry, far afield for us both, pales in comparison to the reaction I get from this, my best anecdote.

I joined the campus anti–nuclear power group when I attended the University of Arizona in the late '70s. One night, as a public meeting with some antinuclear Japanese came to a close, Laurie spread the word among the core group of a party up at Ed Abbey's house. Laurie was our most outgoing member and had recruited Ed to speak at a recent rally. She convinced about ten of us to go to the party.

In retrospect, we were all there probably because Ed had asked Laurie up to his house to "party" and she had misinterpreted the invitation to include the rest of us. In the car on the way there Laurie said she thought Ed had been trying to pick her up, and when we arrived the only party we found was Ed with a bottle of whiskey.

As self-respecting university students we were able to make it into a fairly lively party, with loud music and good, important talk on good, important topics—interspersed with Ed's attempts to hit on Laurie. As for that, her boyfriend stayed close to her all evening; Ed never had a chance.

While Ed was drinking whiskey, I attempted to match him glass for glass. I never had a chance.

Kathy, my girlfriend at the time, was the only other woman at the party. Kathy was an athletic pre-med student who played on the university volleyball team. She had broken her glasses that week and if she really needed to see would put on her "combat glasses"—those swimming goggle-looking devices that strap all the way around your head.

I told her a little too often that they made her look like an insect.

Anyway, the drinks caught up with me. I passed out under Ed's dining room table. It's a cliché but true nonetheless: Ed Abbey drank me under the table.

I awoke to see Ed kissing my girlfriend. Feeling absolutely no jealousy at the time, I got to my feet and groggily beheld them standing intertwined. "How can he kiss her while she's wearing those god-awful glasses?" was the only thought that could fit in my throbbing brain.

I staggered outside to vomit on the driveway, unable to say anything but my home address, which I was reported to have repeated over and over and over until my friends took me home. The next day I woke in my own bed amazed and grateful to find Kathy there.

We talked—those were the pre-AIDS days of open marriages and whatnot—and resumed the talk after she had dinner with Ed the next week. She said Abbey had asked her to come live with him that summer in a forest fire lookout tower in southern Utah. Kathy declined. She told me she thought he was just a dirty old man and she had decided to never even read any of his books.

Kathy went off to a summer of working in a factory watching machines put the latest variety of sugar-coated cereal into waxed-paper bags inside cardboard boxes; she never returned to my life. Ed went to southern Utah alone and I think that was the year he met Clarke, who would become his wife.

I wish I could say I learned enough not to drink whiskey

with Ed Abbey, but there was the time I went to his house with the editor and publisher of the *Tucson Weekly* and some folks from one of Abbey's writing classes. That's another story.

Bill Hoy

On a December morning in 1968, I leaned wearily on my side of the information desk at the visitor center, interpretive and administrative hub of Organ Pipe Cactus National Monument in southwest Arizona. The morning suddenly brightened when a man and woman, too young for the retired set that inhabited the monument during the winter months, came in. They approached the desk looking friendly, perhaps a little apprehensive. For some reason that I've forgotten, I smiled, extended my hand and said simply, "Ed Abbey." Ed, displaying his broad, disarming grin, shook hands and replied with equal brevity, "Yep. My wife, Judy."

It turned out, happily, that we would both share the same quarters for the winter, a lonely, patched-up World War II Quonset hut, located pleasantly far from any government housing or other development.

Our work season was interesting enough, especially after work hours. We both received assorted company that was, in understatement, colorful, particularly that on the Abbey side. I remember one set of guests (the Abbeys') who arrived in a sedan with the sign "peace and love" sloppily emblazoned on each side. While park rangers scoured the monument looking for the suspect "hippie car," the fugitive vehicle remained safely parked at our Quonset.

Judy Abbey, a kind and compassionate girl from New Jersey, was in and out, spending the winter pursuing a master's degree from the University of Arizona.

Ed's job was better than mine. I remained eternally con-
demned to the information desk from which I found release
only long enough to present morning nature walks and evening nature slide programs. Ed, on the other hand, pulled
duty at the campground. He recalled in *Cactus Country*,
"wearing my sharpest Smoky Bear suit, I greeted the camping public, collected fees, kept records and collated statistics,
provided elementary guide service and occasional first aid—
and kidnapped rattlesnakes." His favorite job, however, was
"patrol . . . the privilege of wandering the trails and back-
roads of desert, mountain and borderlands, all within the
boundaries of Organ Pipe."

I remember his daily 5 P.M. reemergence into the visitor
center. After a day of campground duty, he came in silent,
walking with a slight stoop, head down and uncommunica-
tive, wearing a tidy uniform. When he came in following a
day of road patrol, he wore a field uniform invariably sprin-
kled with fine dust, and there was a spring to his step as he
walked erect into the ranger office and dutifully wrote his
patrol report. Road patrol consisted of driving the monument's enormous webbing of rocky and dusty roads and
walking what passed for the monument's only real hiking
trail. In his official line of duty, he picked up litter, cleaned
outhouses, emptied garbage cans, checked weather stations
and contacted (ever so briefly) occasional knots of park visitors. Unofficially, he scanned the hills with binoculars for
wildlife, peered into old hand-dug wells and abandoned mine
shafts, and studied the locomotion systems of crawling creatures. Once he climbed stony 3,415-foot Pinkly Peak and re-
trieved from its summit a "dried out hulk of brown pelican,"
and then asked himself (in *Cactus Country*), "What's a pelican doing up here?"

We valued immensely our two lieu days each week and

spent many of them in the company of our fellow employees, often making forays throughout the region, known historically as Northwest Papagueria. We slipped and slid up and down the ball-bearing slopes of the Pinacate volcanic field, drove the 130-mile historic trek, dubbed the Camino del Diablo, that bisects today's Cabeza Prieta Game Refuge; crawled up high-angle flanks of Baboquivari Peak and the even steeper walls of Montezuma's Head. On long hikes we cajoled each other and shouted repartees along our ranks.

My fondest memory of Ed? Surely it was around those evening campfires. We cooked supper and made camp. After dinner we built up the fire and talked quietly of our concerns, but these concerns were always of the land, never mind under whose jurisdiction it lay.

I remember Ed, on more than one such campfire, sitting with us, the kaleidoscopic shadows and lights flickering on his face. Sometimes there was the wit accompanied by the Abbeyesque grin. But when he talked of the land, he seldom smiled. His head was usually bowed and furrows creased his forehead as he told us of his worries and looked up for our responses. We discovered that he did not worry about the land with his typewriter the way he did with us around the campfire. Those were very good days.

R. H. Ring

How to best remember Ed Abbey? Other than just by remembering him, of course. Get yourself outside. Take a walk, take a hike, take a float down some lonely forgotten river. Take a day off, break the routine, break out of your cubicle, your station on the assembly line, break into yourself. Get away from all those people and straight lines. Take an Ed Abbey Day, tell the boss that's exactly what and why it is.

Take an Abbey Year. Do it your way or don't do it. Tell somebody, anybody, what you really think. Tell everybody. Talk to
a canyon, a sunrise, a cactus—and listen. Get blisters planting a mesquite tree with a pick and shovel against rocks and
caliche under the desert sun. Take some shade and let that
tree grow and let it throw feathery shade for anybody who
happens by for a long, long time. Don't settle for being com-
fortable or reasonable, don't be cool. Admit your gutful of
anger about the mugging, the slow strangulation of the
planet in front of billions of witnesses. Do something about
it. Do more. Shoot your refrigerator. Shoot your TV. Shoot
your phone. Reload. Cut down a billboard. Begin a little road
unconstruction of your own. Do what you can, and make
sure you have. When it's your turn to die, let it happen and
don't give yourself up to the med-technocrats for a few more
dribbling days or hours or years of life on their terms. Stick
it out, stick it in, stick it up. Get in the way of things. Don't be
anybody's unit. Go around intellectually barefoot. Feel the
world with your toes. Lie down with your back flat on warm
bedrock and open your eyes to the impossible sky. Take a
good look around. Shake hands with any old rock. Shake
hands with the moon. Thumb it all off. Live your life.

How best to respect the man and what he stood for, now
that he's gone? Create a park. Rather, since nothing like that
can be created, unless it's already there, just put the name
on some patch of desert he would have liked for its cursed-
ness. There are various possibilities. The city of Tucson just
opened a park in the foothills of the Tucson Mountains
barely a couple miles south of where he lived and died—
about the only city park that's been allowed to remain more
or less natural desert, now called Greasewood Park, a pretty
good name, but not as good, not as evocative as it could be.
Or just a few miles west of where he last was, Saguaro Na-

tional Monument has plans to expand with a new visitors center and trails and what-all—another good place, his kind of land, not easy, not soft, useless. It wouldn't have to be, as they say, developed. Just a sign inviting bullet holes and a path leading off until it disappeared and the desert took over. Just a place to go and get away: Ed Abbey Park.

W. David Laird

At the entry for February 22, 1989, in the slot for lunch my desk calendar reads "Abbey—Big A." That was the last time I saw him. The Big A is an Abbey kind of place: the seating isn't exactly comfort city but the burgers are large (and larger), cooked to order, not served with secret sauce, there's beer on tap, the lighting is dim enough to give a feeling of the privacy of a well-lit cave, and the decor fairly screams that yuppies need not bother.

That's where I saw him first too. I didn't save my desk calendars for my first few years in Tucson, but memory says it was early spring of 1975. Lawrence Clark Powell was the host. I remember writing on that calendar "Edward Abbey!!" The exclamation points added to punctuate the excitement of a bookish, young(er) librarian about to meet one of his heroes.

It would stretch the credulity of anyone who knew Ed to say that we took to each other. Ed didn't take to people, he tolerated them, mostly, and sometimes developed a fondness that was rarely expressed, especially to the person. But I took to him. Ed Abbey, the person, was so different, I thought, from Ed Abbey the writer—different and more interesting because less accessible.

At that first lunch with bookman/librarian Powell at hand to reinforce the message, I suggested that the University

Library would be an excellent repository for papers, man-uscripts, letters and stuff produced by Edward Abbey. I admitted that Special Collections was not an ideal place for storage of one's lifework, but I gushed about the new library nearly completed and due to open soon. Special Collections, I said, will have a place of honor, its own front entrance, climate-controlled stacks for the best possible protection of archives. Abbey, I said, would not be the only important writer in the collection. We would aggressively seek the pa-pers of other writers. Over the years Abbey's papers would form an important part of that "critical mass" that is needed to attract scholars and students to investigate and understand the desert's literary blooming.

Because I do not remember his first response, I am con-vinced it was a less-than-enthusiastic mumble. Not pre-sumptuous about the value of his writings, he said to me some months later as I was loading some boxes of his material into my car, "You really think someone is going to use this stuff?" I assured him someone would. Over the years on a couple of occasions I visited his home and hauled away a box or two of typescripts or letters or anything he was ready to release. On several occasions he called me to say, "Some-where in one of those boxes is. . . . Get it out and make a copy for me, will you? My agent says someone will pay to include it in a collection of. . . ." And I would get it and make a copy. So Ed and I became the first users of his collection. Then we would have lunch—usually at the Big A, for we never found a place we both liked better.

During that last lunch we talked of the novel just finished. "What's it called?" I asked. "*Hayduke Lives!*" he said. "Does he get to blow up the dam?" I asked. "It's a better novel than that," was his enigmatic reply. "What do you mean?" I asked. "I know how to write, now," he said. Indeed, he did.

In the parking lot after that last lunch together I asked about another "shipment" for the Abbey archives. "I guess I've got some stuff." We agreed that I would call. I would go out to his place with my truck. I hadn't managed to make that phone call when word came he had died. At home, not in a hospital—that's important.

Charles Bowden

He couldn't seem to leave town. As Tucson grew larger and more grotesque, he kept talking about going to Moab or Ajo or somewhere. He told me once that Tucson was easy to leave—he'd done it six times. But he never seemed quite able to go through with it, any more than I can. And so now he's dead and still in Tucson.

I had lunch with him a week or so ago at the Big A on Speedway—an Abbey kind of place with the air rich with the scent of seared red meat, the tables dotted with coeds and the walls unchanging over the decades—a brief refuge from Tucson's lucrative cannibalism of its soul. As usual, he admonished me to "get out of that silly magazine," get back into the desert with a pack on my back. And then he shoved forward a pile of books I must read—he always showed up with books he wanted to share. He spoke softly and with a slight smile on his face. The enemy of every government on Earth, the bogeyman of squads of developers, the man seemingly crazed with saving every scrap of wild ground—well, the same guy laughed a lot and seemed to coast through the day fascinated and amused by the absurdity of life, including his own. Whenever I was around him, I was absolutely convinced that he was younger than I ever could be. I'd get kind of mad because he seemed to be having more fun than I was.

This time lunch was about a novel—not about one he

wrote (he never seemed to talk about his own work), but a thick book by some guy in Maryland named Bruce Duffy, titled *The World as I Found It*. He pushed it eagerly toward me and explained it was about philosophers Ludwig Wittgenstein, Bertrand Russell, G. E. Moore and the tong wars of early logical positivism. I allowed that it all sounded as exciting as having my teeth drilled, but he would have none of my objections. By God, he'd written the author a fan letter, and I must read the book. And I did, and Ed Abbey was right.

He was not a simple person to consider. He believed in zero population growth and fathered five kids. He was a lifetime member of the National Rifle Association, a one-time Army M.P., a man who advocated destroying bulldozers to save land, tossed his beer cans out the truck window and recently bought an old Cadillac convertible and tooled around town with a sporty cap on his head. He never made a lot of money, he gave 10 percent of his income to environmental causes, and for years and years scrapped along with part-time jobs and kept writing and writing. He hardly seemed to raise his voice, but had logical, coherent fierce opinions. He had an anarchist's contempt for government, and was like a distillate of whatever the word *American* means.

And he could write better than any man or woman I have ever known.

Many have pointed out these traits, and others, as contradictions. They were not. They were Edward Abbey, a bundle of appetites, ideas and delights. Before the last mayoral election he called me up and we had lunch. Ed Abbey had decided to run for mayor—not grunt through a real campaign, but declare for the office and debate Tom Volgy and other contenders. We were sitting down over a plate of machaca when I broke the bad news to him. "Ed, you don't live in the city, you live in the county." He seemed kind of indignant that such a requirement existed and could stop him from his appointed rounds.

The first time I met him, I was out at his house to interview a guest of his for the local paper. I was leery of meeting him, kind of like I was disturbing a national monument. So I tapped timidly on the door. He opened it up, introduced himself and instantly thrust a copy of my first book into my hands—a text that had fallen dead from the press and taken almost ten years to sell two thousand copies. He asked if I would autograph it, and went on and on about its wonders. So he may have had pretty bad literary taste, but he was one of the kindest men I have ever known.

We became friends. And what we did, well, we talked about books and ideas mainly. I don't think I ever spent ten minutes kicking around environmental issues with him—I guess they were simply a given. He worked very hard at his writing. An Abbey draft was blitzkrieged with crossed-out words; clauses and sentences moved and had the general appearance of a bed of writhing serpents. Of course, it read as if he were talking to you, as if he had just dashed it off. He wrote so well that a lot of people did not appreciate the craft in his work—you can crack his books open almost anywhere and just start reading out loud. But if you start looking very closely, you'll find he makes every word work, every sentence, every paragraph. The stuff's as tight as the head of a drum.

Of course, what stopped people like myself in their tracks was not simply his style, it was his mind. He wasn't just an entertainer, he had ideas to sell, and for decades, he explored his ideas, refined them and forced us to snap awake and pay attention. Ed Abbey invented the Southwest we live in. He made us look at it, and when we looked up again we suddenly saw it through his eyes and sensed what he sensed—we were killing the last good place. His words were driven by a moral energy, a biting tongue and, thank God, by an abundant sense of humor. It's pretty hard to read him without laughing out loud. And he was radical. Want to save the National Parks? Get the stinking cars out. Want to keep Arizona beautiful and healthy? Let's make half of it a wilderness. Want to bring the Colorado River back to life? Let's blow up Glen Canyon Dam. There are near twenty books. Read them and see. I suppose his reputation will now fall into the claws of Visigoths of the English departments, and I don't know what they'll make of him. But here's what I think: When I'm dead and dust, people will still be reading Edward Abbey. Because the stuff he wrote is alive.

The morning he died, his wife, Clarke, called me and told me and I felt like a giant hole had been punched in the mind of the Southwest, a kind of new chilling void. And I sensed Tucson and the region had slipped one more ratchet and lost another piece of its dwindling soul. I realized I was going to be a little lonelier for the rest of my life. I don't figure on being lucky enough to know another Ed Abbey.

Then I remembered a letter he wrote to the newspapers—he seemed hardly able to get through a day without firing off a broadside to some newspaper or magazine. He suggested that a suitable memorial should be created for a leading local developer. He wanted to name the Ina Road sewage treatment plant after him. Neither newspaper would publish the letter.

The last time I talked to him, he told me how he'd written an essay a year or so ago in which he'd noted that nobody in his family ever died. And then, suddenly, his brother had died from cancer, his mother had been run over and killed by a truck. He looked up at me with a mad twinkle in his eyes.

I said, "Maybe you ought to print a retraction."

God, I'm going to miss him. Who in the hell is going to keep us honest? The guy we counted on, well, he moved on.

Doug Peacock

Last Saturday, Terry Williams and I took a hike down Millcreek Canyon. Coincidentally, the last time Terry took that hike was with Ed. The last time I took that hike I was also with Ed, back in 1975. Terry said, "Peacock, don't worry about it, you'll find the answer, go walk the rim of Lavender Canyon for five days, and you'll figure out what you're here for." So I did, I picked up that next day and went out to Lavender Canyon and walked the rimrock, climbed up on top, fell down dozens of times, hiked the whole rim buck naked when the weather permitted.

Terry is a lot smarter than I am, so it dawned on me—it actually only took twenty minutes, I just hiked the other five days for the hell of it—that the reason I'm here is that it's not the end, this isn't something you just sign off and close the book on and walk away from. That's why I'm here. . . .

This is not the end, despite the easy wisdom that death is part of the great cycle of life. Ed's going was not exactly a surprise; and, though difficult, it wasn't unlike what he would have wished for himself. But I have to admit to having been floored by the whole experience. I was really paralyzed for weeks, and that's hard for me to admit.

Ed would, of course, have totally disapproved, which finally shook me out of it. He would say, "Douglas, why all this moping around, go do something." So I did.

I have a little note from Peter Matthiessen which I received at my home in Tucson last week. . . . Peter quoted the words of Akaitcho, the warrior, who said to Sir John Franklin, the English polar explorer, in 1824: "If you are determined to go, some of my young men will join the party because it shall not be said that we permitted you to die alone."

And that's close to my heart. Though most of Hayduke is buried under a pile of black rock someplace, his spirit lives on. . . . Without Ed walking point anymore, there is going to be more work for all of us.

I'm simply here to recommit myself to that purpose.

Dave Foreman

I'm Dave Foreman and this [holds a can of Coors 3.2 beer] is supposed to be beer. I once heard Doug Peacock give a speech which he said was going to be a one-beer speech, and when the beer was done he would be finished. Well, for reasons that I will tell you at the end of my presentation, this is going to be a one-Coors speech, which might mean it's a very short speech. [He takes a swig of the beer.] Yeah.

My words, whatever I say today, will seem small and insignificant, reflected in the mirror of Ed Abbey's work. I'm humbled by those of you who gathered together today, by the others who share this podium with me. I am overwhelmed and small by the landscape around us; the Arches, and Devil's Garden, the Book Cliffs, a Single Leaf Ash and Utah Juniper, the cryptogram soil, and Narrow Leaf Yucca.

I am going to persevere and try to make a few comments about Ed, whom I loved more than I can say. First of all, I would like to tell a little story. A number of years ago, right after we started Earth First!, I got a marvelous letter from an old Wobbly, Henry Tom Smith in California, who joined Earth First! in 1981, I believe. He wrote that John Muir spoke to his high school graduating class. And I was just floored. I sat looking at this letter trying to imagine what it would have been like to have seen and heard John Muir in person. And thinking what it would be like to carry that memory with you for your life.

Well, many of us know that. We knew Ed Abbey in person. And I think for those of us who have a year left, or ten years, or fifty years, that that will be a memory to carry and to cherish just like Henry Tom Smith carried his of John Muir. Those of us who saw Ed Abbey, who knew him, who felt his handshake, who shared a cigar or beer with him, have truly been privileged. And so rejoice for that. We have a memory that is unbeatable.

Three little points I would like to make about Ed that may not otherwise be made, and I am happy to see the American flag here beside me because that's one of the points I want to make: that Ed was not a counterculturist. He wasn't an antinomian. He was an American. He knew where he came from. He knew that he was born out of the hillbilly bones of this country—what made him, and what's made all of us. And by being part of this culture, by not denying it, by accepting his place in it; by knowing from whence he came; it made his criticism more incisive, more biting, more trenchant, more important. When we try to deny who we are, when we hate everything about us and what produced us, I think we lose something there. We lose the connection—a feeling, a belonging.

Edward Abbey was a great man. He was a great American. He represented the best of the American dream. He represented what this country could have become, had it not turned its back on its ideals two hundred years ago. I think that is something we need to remember—is that we are Americans like Ed Abbey. By accepting that, we become stronger, and our criticism of the prostitution of America becomes more powerful.

The second point I would like to make is that Ed Abbey

received a great deal of criticism from people who did not understand him—who did not know what he was talking about. And I remember twenty years ago, living on the Zuni Reservation, going to Shalako on a frozen December evening and watching the Mudhead Kachinas. In all primal cultures there are forces like the Mudhead Kachinas, the tricksters, who, while the most sacred ceremonies are going on, are making fun. It's as though you would have a group of nuns and priests up there in St. Peter's Square while the Pope was giving an Easter sermon, making obscene gestures. And that's important in every real society this planet has ever seen. We have had to laugh at our most sacred ideas. At our most honored personages.

[He takes another swallow of beer.] I can't speak very well with a Coors.

Ed Abbey was the Mudhead Kachina of the environmental movement. Ed Abbey was the Mudhead Kachina of the whole social change movement in this country. And it's to our everlasting shame as idealists that more of us did not understand that. Ed was a trickster farting in polite company. Pissing on overblown egos, making a caricature of himself and laughing at himself. Laughing at all of us because we all have to do that. Ed was the wise prophet from the desert that tried to keep us on track and to not take ourselves too seriously.

The third point I want to make is that Ed once said, and I think he wrote it in several places, that one brave deed is worth a thousand books. He's disparaging his own contribution. But every book of Ed Abbey's, every essay, every story has launched a thousand brave deeds. How do you evaluate that kind of contribution, that kind of magic that he possessed?

All we can do for that is to continue to be motivated. For

each of us to go out and commit those brave deeds in honor of Ed. Whether they are writing for the puny 5.1-million-acre Utah State Wilderness Proposal, or the 16-million-acre Earth First! Wilderness Proposal for Utah; whether it's going out and putting a wrench in Cal Black's latest development; whether it's farting in polite company, let's be inspired to do those brave deeds. That's the only legacy that we can return to Ed.

C. L. RAWLINS

Elegy

for Edward Abbey

I'd like to say that coyotes passed the word along,
that leafless willows dreamed it up the roots of cottonwood
and sage along each muddy stream. I'd like to say the
    Colorado
told the Green, the Escalante, the San Juan, that grief
rose up each tributary to the melting snow.

Or that he sat out on some overlook, apart,
the sunset flaring up behind a blue-dark roll of storm,
composed a final question as the gust-front tugged his
    sleeve
and caught a bolt—the years of pain condensed, a flash.
That thunder punched the windows out.

In Bluff and Blanding, every door kicked open
with the blast, walls suddenly uncertain, fences hung and
    buried,
every shiny scrap discarded on the desert plucked and
    howling homeward
on that wind. That every rimrock shuddered, wept
huge blocks of sandstone, pounding the tattoo.

I'd like to say the wished-for vultures carved
those long bones clean as limestone in the sight of sky.
If words are truth despite our eyes, then I'd say that. The
    father
of our grinning anger's gone; I never knew him better
than in song, the page turned in a thousand lights.

If empty beer cans all fill up with grace
then there's a heaven. Red sand drifts them full
beside the road, abolishes their names, buries them like
    books
with titles worn away by hands, a legacy mysterious
as strata, hidden and revealed: the holy land.

Pretty lies that please the heart are true
to that extent. The desert—no one's place—collects its
    patience,
love, indifference; we don't know. We know our loss, our
    desperation
when the burning space that hiked and pissed and laughed
    fills up
with air, when silence runs it through and through.

West of Arches, Utah

Books by Edward Abbey

The following list excludes books published posthumously, including such notable titles as *Confessions of a Barbarian: Selections from the Journals of Edward Abbey, 1951–1989*, edited with an introduction by David Petersen (Boston: Little, Brown, 1994).

Fiction

Black Sun (1971)
The Brave Cowboy (1960)
Confessions of a Barbarian (1986)
Fire on the Mountain (1962)
The Fool's Progress (1988)
Good News (1980)
Hayduke Lives! (1990)
Jonathan Troy (1959)
The Monkey Wrench Gang (1975)

Nonfiction

Abbey's Road (1979)
Appalachian Wilderness (with Eliot Porter, 1970)
Beyond the Wall (1984)

Cactus Country (with Ernst Haas, 1973)

Desert Images (with David Muench, 1979)

Desert Solitaire (1968)

Down the River (1982)

The Hidden Canyon (with John Blustein, 1977)

The Journey Home (1977)

One Life at a Time, Please (1987)

Slickrock (with Philip Hyde, 1971)

Slumgullion Stew (1985); reprinted as *The Best of Edward Abbey*
(1987)

Vox Clamantis in Deserto: Some Notes from a Secret Journal
(1989)

Books About Edward Abbey

James Bishop. *Epitaph for a Desert Anarchist: The Life and Legacy of Edward Abbey.* New York: Atheneum, 1994.

Garth McCann. *Edward Abbey.* Boise State University Western Writers Series. Boise: Boise State University, 1977.

Spencer Maxwell. *Collecting Abbey: A Checklist of the First Editions of Edward Abbey with Approximate Values and Commentary.* Santa Fe: Vinegar Tom Press, 1991.

Ann Ronald. *The New West of Edward Abbey.* Albuquerque: The University of New Mexico Press, 1982. Reprinted. Reno: The University of Nevada Press, 1987.

———

Thanks to the efforts of the Southwestern bookmen Lawrence Clark Powell and W. David Laird, the Special Collections Division of the University of Arizona Library is the best source of information on Abbey's life and work. In it are housed scores of original manuscripts, notebooks, diaries, screenplays, published pieces, photographs, and letters to and from some of the world's most important writers and musicians, not to mention Robert Redford, Gloria Steinem, the IRS, and the FBI. Laird remembers Abbey's asking incredulously whether he thought anyone would really "use this stuff." The Abbey archives are among the most frequently consulted in the library.